Mornings on the Porch

Nancy Kuykendall

Mornings on the Porch

Nancy Kuykendall

TATE PUBLISHING
AND ENTERPRISES, LLC

Published by Tate Publishing & Enterprises, LLC
127 E. Trade Center Terrace | Mustang, Oklahoma 73064 USA
1.888.361.9473 | www.tatepublishing.com

Tate Publishing is committed to excellence in the publishing industry. The company reflects the philosophy established by the founders, based on Psalm 68:11,
"The Lord gave the word and great was the company of those who published it."

Book design copyright © 2014 by Tate Publishing, LLC. All rights reserved.
Author Photo by Troy D. Gunderson
Cover design by Ivan Charlem Igot
Interior design by Jimmy Sevilleno

Published in the United States of America

ISBN: 978-1-63306-575-8
Family & Relationships / General
14.07.21

Dedicated
to my
dad.

Acknowledgements

Thanks to my dad, J Kenneth Eakins, physician, professor, minister, and author. I am a daughter who has been fortunate to have my dad's love and support throughout my life. His encouragement, rather than shocked disbelief, when I told him I was going to write is a precious gift. It is my dad who gave me a love for books. One special summer, he opened the door to reading for me, supplying me with wonderful classics to read then present to him an oral report. I was struggling with reading, but his insight to provide me with good books and stories that touched me got me hooked, and I have read ever since. My dad has been my teacher and example since day one.

Thanks to my husband, Steve, my best friend, who seems to believe I am capable of accomplishing anything. His gift of encouragement, of which I have been the recipient for as long as I've known him, has spurred me on many times. His belief in me has seen me through much and helped me believe in myself.

Thanks to my children Jason, Ryan, and Amy, who have each inspired me with their own journeys and strengths. They are my heroes in so many ways. Each has given me their love, and their very existence has always inspired me to be the best I can be.

Thanks to my siblings, Doug and wife Debbie, Sheri and Laurie, who did not laugh when I announced my starting this project. They have proven their love.

Thanks and gratitude to those who served as readers: my dad, J. Kenneth Eakins; my daughter, Amy Hatcher; Don Winton; Bill and Jean Hagler; Tina Kleinhaus; Lisa and Hanna Staley; and Dave and Candy McDowell. Your generosity in time and effort in reading my stories, giving them thought, and giving feedback was helpful beyond measure. Thank you for your time and energy, thoughts and helpful remarks.

Thank you to Tate Publishing for the opportunity to share my thoughts with others and for all their efforts in bringing my book to its final product.

Thanks be to God for his loving kindness and care and for traveling this road with me as he set me on this path to begin with. Truly, all things are possible with God.

Contents

Introduction

I am not a writer. At least I wasn't. I remember slaving over high school and college papers, even being brought to tears, struggling to fulfill the writing assignments given. I liked writing letters. I liked writing poems and songs. I often expressed myself in those ways but somehow the freedom I felt, in expressing my thoughts and feelings through those rhyming verses and music, was lost when I went to write a story or any other paper. I sought out tutoring to get me through a college freshman English class. The teacher was a published author, knew her craft and had high expectations of her students. The tutoring helped and I passed the class, barely. I believed I had no ability to write and I really never thought much about it again.

I have been a musician my entire adult life. I first studied music at age ten and by the time I was an adult

I delved into music much further—studying music, teaching music and performing music. I have expressed myself through various instruments and singing. I married a musician. My life has been very much about music.

It took me quite some time to take my tiny seeds of thought and actually apply them pen to paper. I really didn't know why I should undertake such a project or journey. I dismissed the thought of writing more than once. All I could think of were the many red marks scribbled all over my college papers ... all the errors and low grades. Thoughts that did not breed confidence. But the thought kept coming to me and stories started to bang on the wall of my brain. I would find myself writing stories in my mind as I took my morning walks or went about daily chores. I kept noticing repeating stories ... stories that would not go away. I kept hearing the same voice telling me to write them down and I wanted to, but what about all those red marks? One day I stopped dead in my tracks, suddenly aware of the voice again and said, "Lord is that you? Are you telling me to write? Me?" I learned long ago it is better to say "yes" to God than "no", and always to my benefit.

As I came to the conclusion that I would write these stories, it seemed impossible to me that I, of all people, should attempt this challenge, but maybe I actually could write them. I got excited about it. The stories were begging to be told. Stories of daily experiences. Stories of deep emotion. Stories of special moments or special people or special pets. Stories of usual things with no real significance that came to have special significance. Stories that seemed ordinary but ended up extraordinary, at least to me. Stories that kept asking to be told, though I had no certain reason why. Why these stories? The why wasn't for me to know. If the stories were to be told then God would equip me. God would give me the know-how and he would know the why. If the stories found in these pages speak to you, the reader, then I am even more thrilled, than I already have been, that I took this journey laid before me.

—Nancy

An Extraordinary Morning

The day started like any other. Most of my mornings resemble each other. I awoke semi-early, after dawn. I'm not an early riser, but I don't sleep in late easily either. I quietly grabbed my exercise clothes and walking shoes, which I had laid out the night before. I dressed and left my husband to his slumber since he didn't need to be up just yet. I have had this routine for years, getting in a good walk, or run, first thing in the morning. I have found that if I don't exercise first thing, it's not likely to happen at all. My piano teaching schedule allows me long, quiet mornings since my teaching is done in the afternoons and early evenings when both children and adults are available. I have most always walked alone and have never minded the solitude. Actually, I enjoy it. I don't seem to need a partner to get me motivated and out the door. I enjoy the time to think through my day and ponder various issues. It's also my best time to talk with God. So as usual, I struck out on my walk, expecting nothing in particular. I would pass by the same businesses, same houses, then enter the city trail if I so chose.

I walked down our street, just a couple of small blocks, when something unusual occurred. As I passed by a city worker struggling with some sort of grate on the sidewalk, I offered my standard "Good morning." He looked up and greeted me with a big smile and very cheery "Good morning! How are you today?" I was taken aback by his smile and the cheeriness in his voice. It was still fairly early, and this was not a usual response. More commonly, I received a grunt or an almost inaudible, obligatory returned greeting. I was so stunned I stopped in my tracks for a slight moment, returned the smile, answered that I was just fine, and wished him a good day. He gave a cheery response, and I walked on, marveling at such a nice encounter. An unusual encounter.

As I walked on, I approached a somewhat-busy corner. There are stop signs at the opposing sides of a throughway and no crosswalk for pedestrians. Often a driver sitting at the stop sign and wanting to turn left will have to wait a bit. If a pedestrian comes along, the driver may wait even longer, having to let the slow-moving pedestrian cross. It was my habit to wave to drivers wanting to turn left, and I would cross the street behind their car so as not to hold them up and make them miss the break in traffic that would allow them to turn. Understanding the left-hand-turn dilemma at this corner, as I approached and saw a driver waiting for a break in traffic and seeing me approach on foot, I motioned him to go ahead. It was a simple gesture, yet in the brief instant that he realized he'd be able to turn, rather than wait for me then have to wait further for another break in traffic, he shot me a quick wave and large grateful smile. Again, I was struck by the cheery smile and friendly exchange that had just occurred, though no words were spoken. Most often, drivers are not so appreciative and just want pedestrians out of their way. This driver was different. I considered how, in just minutes, I had had two friendly morning encounters with complete strangers.

I walked on, pondering these nice exchanges. Most of those I pass and greet are not so friendly. "The younger the person, the less friendly" as a general rule. I've often thought about this while walking and greeting others as we pass. Most don't make eye contact or speak. Our society has, for some time, taught children not to speak to strangers. Though I understand the dangers facing children and our society as a whole, it always saddens me when a child on his or her way to school will not look up, let alone accept or speak a greeting. I have often offered a "Hello" or "Good morning" or "Have a nice day," only to be totally ignored as if we had not passed by each other on the same sidewalk at all. Most school children passing by are sullen, if not just plain fearful of an approaching stranger. I often wonder what their lives are like and if they have any of the carefree feeling I had as a child. The very youngest children, still in strollers, will often grin and give a child's wave. They have not yet learned to be afraid. I walked on.

I was walking and thinking about the fearful unfriendliness of children, and people in general, when I suddenly met up with a tiny puppy tending a garden with his owner. The owner smiled and assured me her pup was friendly, which was immediately proven by his wagging tail and appreciation of a few pats on his head. The dog's owner and I chatted a minute; she shared how she came to have such a fine little dog. The conversation was very pleasant, and I walked on, counting that so far I had, had three very lovely encounters with complete strangers, four if you count the pup. It felt nice. It felt like a gift. I wandered on.

As I reached the end of our long street and made the left hand turn necessary to enter the trail, I caught sight of an older gentleman watering his lawn. He offered me a smile and wave from across the street. We had never met and never spoken. Being out of speaking range, I simply returned both gestures. How nice it was of him to greet me rather than ignore me. I suddenly felt I was living in *Mister Rogers' Neighborhood* where everyone is a friendly neighbor. I started singing the familiar song, "It's a beautiful day in the neighborhood…" Today, everyone was my friend and neighbor.

I decided to skip the trail and head toward home, back the way I came, but down another street. I didn't know it, but the surprises hadn't ended yet. I was already feeling happy and that the day was good, enchanted by how much good will I had encountered on a rather short walk so far. I was thinking about this when I suddenly heard a large and noisy truck approaching. I glanced up as it was passing me by and preparing to stop at the stop sign. What did I see? I actually did a double take. The driver was smiling at me and gave a nod of his head as a greeting! What? It may seem an overreaction, but I was dumbfounded! How often does that happen? I smiled back as he made his quick stop and went on his way. I stopped for a moment and glanced around myself to see if all these friendly people were seeing something I was not. I had a quick thought that maybe there was something stuck to my clothing and some sort of joke was being played. However, I found and saw nothing to substantiate that thought, and my peacefulness returned. I mentioned earlier that my walking time is often my time to speak with God. I suddenly felt God was speaking to me. It felt as if he were saying, "Good morning" and greeting me with love and smiles through those he'd put in my path, including the puppy. I smiled to myself at that thought and wondered what I might have done to be so deserving of such a special morning. Nothing. I couldn't think of a single reason, except sometimes God just pours out extra love on his children.

I walked on toward home. I looked at the houses I passed, especially interested in the porches of each. Our neighborhood is old, with individual and unique houses, most with porches large enough to comfortably sit on. Ours was the same, and I was anticipating sitting on my own porch as I did each morning after my walk. I passed a house with a woman enjoying her morning coffee and paper on her porch. I would soon be home caressing my cup of dark, hot cocoa, as I did every morning. Not being a coffee drinker, I enjoy my hot chocolate. The woman and I gave each other a little wave, and I called out to her that I'd soon be doing the same on my porch. She smiled. Each house I passed, I wondered about those inside. I said hello to their cats, patiently waiting by the door to be let in. Even the cats were friendly that morning; some wanting attention, and some at least not running away in fear.

As I approached my own house, I was eager to tell my husband about my walk and all the friendly encounters. He had gotten up and was preparing to go to work. In some ways, it seemed like no big deal, but I was beaming and excited. It was not a usual morning, though when I first stepped out the door, I had no reason to believe it would be different than any other morning. I started the tea kettle water on the stove for my hot cocoa. I took my devotional books and writing materials to the porch. As I prepared to read and also write a few letters, I thought about God's love and how sometimes he just surprises us with the nicest gifts. On this morning, it was the gift of friendliness and good will, which is so often missing in our daily lives. It meant something to me. God knew it would. I had the feeling that, while I slept, he had met with some angels and devised this beautiful plan to bless me that particular morning. Have you ever felt a special love from God? I did that morning. It was an extraordinary morning.

The Angels on Easter Eve

I was on my way. I couldn't believe I was actually going. I was still seething with fury at the great offense I felt and had been harboring. There have been very few times in my life when I felt as angry, offended, and invalidated as I did over this situation. I still didn't understand why it was handled as it was, and I still hadn't forgiven the offender. Funny thing, the offender and I had never even met, only spoken once on the phone. I was dealing with this anger and hurt feelings as I drove to the little café where I was to play my last piano gig this Saturday evening. I had been dropped from the rotation of musicians. The café owner had no idea I was so upset.

I had been playing piano at this café for about a year, providing dinner music for two hours, usually the first Saturday night of each month. Musician friends of ours plus a trio my husband was in had been on the rotation a long time. I always went to listen and often was invited to sit in on a song or two, either playing bass guitar or singing. I enjoyed that the guys so readily accepted me and included me. Being mainly a piano player, I had decided to approach the café owner with the idea of including a night of soft piano music in her line up of musicians. It would be different, a change from all the rock, jazz, and pop groups she had performing each weekend. I was hoping she would go for the idea. She did! She had not met me nor ever heard me, but she decided to give it a try. I had my chance to do what I do and offer something different, instrumental piano music, to her patrons. I took the Saturday nights she offered. It had been fairly successful, I thought, from comments I had received from both customers and the employees serving them.

So here I was, driving over for the last time, car packed with my keyboard, amp, and music binder. I was angry at how I had been dismissed, and dismissed so easily. I had considered not even showing up, sort of giving the same treatment I had received. However, I couldn't do it, maybe out of manners, maybe out of pride, or maybe out of pure stubbornness. I'm not certain which, maybe all three, but I was feeling insulted and was at the point of tears the entire drive over. I felt ignored and cast off. I prayed, asking God to calm me down and replace my bitterness with grace and the ability to carry on and share my music on this night. I was so worked up I was afraid I might be rude to the first person who challenged me. Usually, at least one person (it has always been a man) would make a rude remark. Tonight, I felt I might be quite rude back if I encountered such a person.

Through the years, I had discovered that most people enjoy hearing something more upbeat, more pop rock, than instrumental piano music. I had also discovered that most want to hear music and songs they already know. Anything new seems to be boring or unacceptable to many. This is something I do not understand. I certainly do not find myself falling into either category, quite the opposite actually, but one thing I have learned about myself is that I am very often in the minority in many areas of life. With music, I enjoy hearing unfamiliar tunes, and I enjoy seeking out new pieces I do not know. I have fallen in love with many songs and pieces of music by discovering something new. Still the piano was not on the top of most people's favorite nor was what I most enjoyed playing. So I had these two counts against me already. I would be playing instrumental piano music, and I would be playing mostly unfamiliar tunes. It was quite possible that someone would call out asking why I didn't play something else or be like some other artist they know and like. I find that extremely offensive, not just as a musician, but as a person. It is not so different from approaching a stranger and asking them why they don't style their hair differently or dress differently. I would never approach a musician and ask them to be someone other than they are. Taking requests is one thing, but being asked to play like or be like someone else, as has happened to me, is very unacceptable to my way of thinking. On one particular night, when it was said to me that I should liven it up and play some Little Richard, I simply remarked that I was there to play dinner music and nicely told the gentleman to eat his dinner and enjoy the music. It reminded me of the night a classic rock band my husband was in was playing for a Christmas party, and a group of guests insistently called out, "Play country." They were so annoying that I finally approached them and suggested that if they wanted a country band then a country band should have been hired. I have little patience for such rudeness. Maybe my feelings are common to most, or maybe I am extra sensitive, but I do not tolerate such behavior well. On this night, when I was already feeling such anger, I was afraid of what I may say to one I considered rude. Again, I prayed for patience and for relief from my indignation.

I drove on wondering why I had been treated with so little respect. It seemed that throughout the year when I had contacted the café owner, I would have to wait days for a reply, whereas my husband and others seemed to hear back almost immediately. Since the owner and I had never met, since her employees were giving her positive remarks regarding me and the piano music, and since there were no negative encounters, I did not understand why I was so ignored, or so I felt. Then came the phone call that pricked my emotions and started this tantrum I'd been having ever since. I retrieved a message from our answering machine, a machine that has my voice on it and is a home number for both my husband and me. The café owner identified herself and spoke directly, and only to my husband, in her message, though the message greatly had to do with me as well. She was filling in her calendar and asking my husband if his band could take certain dates and then included asking them to take a Saturday I was already slated to play. She admitted in her message that she knew I was scheduled for that night but wanted something more upbeat (those dreaded words) and asked if they could also take that night. Never once was the message directed toward me. Never once did she address me, and no apology given. I was simply replaced. As is sometimes the case in my life, I felt invisible. Adding insult to injury was that I had been usurped by my own husband and friends, who gladly took my gig date. I was indignant. I understood that they were just trying to stay in the owner's good graces and accommodate her, but in the process, I and my feelings were simply erased. I did not take kindly to it, and I expressed myself to the band taking my place. They laughed it off, chalking it up to the music business and didn't really realize how deeply her simple dismissal affected me. I had gotten that gig on my own accord. I had played that gig steadily. I had lived up to all that was expected of me. I had been appreciated by at least some listeners. I was then let go, with the owner never once speaking to me directly—not then and not ever. I had vowed not to attend their gig the night that would have been mine; but in the end, I did go, and I even sang with them a few times. I decided it was better for me to keep my face out there. Maybe pride again. Maybe just business savvy in the music arena. I was still pondering it all—my feelings and dealing with how to get through this, my last night. I asked God to make my music matter to someone. That was the thing. I wanted it to matter.

I arrived at the café. On this night, I would be playing inside, as it was still too cool for being outside on the patio, where we all performed during warm weather. I parked in the spot designated for musicians. I began unloading my gear. There was a small crowd. I noticed a few couples sitting at tables for two and a table with four diners. The party of four sat in front of and just to the side of where I was to set up. It was a gentleman and three women. I learned later the gentleman was with his wife, and they had two visiting friends. As could be expected, the gentleman almost immediately asked me what I would be playing. I was so on guard that I really didn't appreciate his inquiry. He'd find out soon enough what I'd be playing and that it would pretty much be nothing he would recognize. I kept my tongue and answered his question. He didn't believe me that he would probably not know most of what I played. He then asked what my first song would be. I explained it would be an original instrumental piece that my husband and I had co-written, again unfamiliar to him. He commented he was eager to hear it, but I detected a bit of judgment and challenge in his tone. Maybe it was just my defensive mood.

I finished setting up and began to play, starting with the original composition. I made a medley out of it by going directly into another piece that was not an original. When I completed the medley and stopped briefly to begin another piece, the gentleman commented that he enjoyed what he heard so far. Hmmm. I took a mental note. He had given what seemed a genuinely positive comment. I played on.

I played that first hour, just flipping through the pages of my binder. They were pieces compiled from my many books. Occasionally, I played an original composition. Music, especially the act of playing music, can be an emotional release and quite cathartic. I was feeling better little by little as I played piece after piece. Furthermore, I was noticing that the diners seemed to be enjoying the music. The group in front of me, specifically the gentleman, had no negative comments. They even clapped a few times and said, "Nice." A table of two had been smiling and clapping after most every piece. They let me know they were enjoying the music. I was pleasantly surprised. It wasn't that I had never been shown such appreciation. I had. But I had arrived feeling defeated, inconsequential, and wasn't expecting much support. After all, I had been let go. With the friendliness and support of those there, I began to feel a bit more at ease and not so ready to fight. I continued to play the music of my choice then took my ten-minute break. Seeing I was on break, a couple called me over to their table. I approached them, just a bit on guard, but to my relief, they expressed how much they had been enjoying the music while they ate and visited with each other. They asked when I would be back, explaining they wanted to bring their parents, who they knew would enjoy what I was playing. I had to inform them that, unfortunately, it was my last night and that the owner decided to nix the piano in favor of more upbeat music. I thanked them for their compliment and then encouraged them to call the café and let the owner know how much they enjoyed the piano music if they'd like to see it continue. I have no idea if they, or anyone else, ever called.

Somewhat encouraged, I returned to my bench and began playing the second and last hour. I was feeling better, but I was still feeling defeated. It just seemed I couldn't let it go. I had already been dealing with this for weeks, and it seemed I should get over it, but it went deeper than just being let go from this rotation. It conjured up deeper feelings that stemmed from the public's general dislike of piano music, at least in this circle of performing musicians and their friends and followers. I took it personally. I so often find myself lost somewhere between the pop rock group and the classical music group, being active in both in my community. I don't quite fully fit into either group like some hybrid that hasn't quite found full acceptance on either side for my particular style and strengths. Nevertheless, the music I play best expresses myself and who I am, and I believed in being true to it while joining in other types of music as well. I refused to give up and erase myself.

The hour was passing, and I was nearly done for the night. I had settled in well and was enjoying playing to the small but appreciative crowd. So far, I had not received one negative comment or rude remark. "Amazing!" I thought. "This is a good night." Little did I know how marvelous it was about to become.

I had about fifteen minutes to go and was just starting a piece when an older couple walked in, smiling broadly, with the husband, I assumed, boldly announcing they had come to hear the piano player. I was so stunned I almost stopped playing. I looked closely at this couple. Had I ever seen them before? I didn't recognize them at all. Had they read the placard that listed the schedule of musicians and come because they enjoyed piano music? They seemed especially interested in me, yet I could not place them. They didn't say they knew me or act as if I should know them. The man simply stated they came to hear the piano player. He didn't say they came to hear the piano music. He said they came to hear the piano player. It felt personal in some way. They took a seat at a table directly in front of me and ordered iced tea.

I was especially aware of the husband, his wife sitting behind him. He smiled and drank his tea calmly and serenely and clapped after each piece I played, smiling broadly all the while. I kept wondering just who this man was while I enjoyed playing for him. I was about to play one of my very favorite pieces by one of my very favorite contemporary composers and told him so as I started the piece. It was a prelude in F major. I so enjoy expressing myself through that piece, and I so enjoyed playing it for him. He had been listening intently all the while continuing to smile. He seemed to enjoy the music. I played the last note, held it, and released it. The man in front of me, smiled so brightly and clapped so appreciatively, and then said, "That was beautiful! You know, you should continue playing what you love so much and play it because you love it." For me, the world stopped at that moment. Before I knew it, I had jumped up from my bench and went to him, happy tears stinging my eyes. I touched him lightly on the arm and said, "Sir, you and what you just said to me are an exact answer to prayer. A prayer I prayed on my way here tonight. Thank you!" He simply smiled at me. I thanked him again and went back to my keyboard because I still had a few minutes to fill to complete my job and earn my pay, plus I felt like playing. Joy and confidence had returned to me in that instant.

As I was about to start, the husband and wife rose from their seats, and he said they needed to leave to get to a prayer service. It being the night before Easter and having previously been pianist at a Catholic church for a few years, I asked if they were attending an Easter vigil mass. With a smile, he said, "No, just a prayer service." He gave a wave, and as I started my last piece, I watched them walk out the door, and I wondered who they were. The direction they walked was out of my view, except for a few feet. I could not see them walking away, but as a warmth spread through me, I had the distinct feeling that they simply dissipated and vanished up into heaven. I had a very strong, unexplainable feeling that these two were angels! Angels who were going to be in a prayer "service" in heaven that night. Angels sent directly to me and for me on this Easter Eve. Angels sent in direct answer to my prayers and struggles. Angels sent to encourage me and validate me. Angels sent especially to me by God to let me know I was doing all right and I was musically being who I was created to be. I was appreciated and even enjoyed. Angels sent directly for me that night to shower me with God's love. The next day was Easter, and my joy had returned! I had a great night, my last night playing at that café.

I have been back to that café many times since that night, both to hear other musicians and to perform there myself with a six-piece band that my husband and I are both in. I have never seen that couple again, though at first, I would watch for them. I saw them only once, the Easter Eve when two angels were sent to comfort me and bless me.

The Man on the Corner

I can't remember if it was a Friday, my usual day off, or a Saturday, but I had gone to visit a friend in a neighboring city. It was a thirty-minute drive from my home to hers. I made the trek to her house that day for lunch and a visit. It was more common for her to come visit me because we lived in the city and she lived in the country. Her trips into town to shop brought her my way more often than my trips her way.

That's one reason she usually came to visit me. Another is that I don't like to drive, at least not on freeways. I avoid them like the plague. I am quite simply afraid of traffic and high speeds. But I loved my friend, felt it was fair and also my responsibility to go her direction once in a while, plus I enjoyed her home. I did tell her that she should feel quite special knowing I braved the freeway just for her. She laughed and said she was glad I did. In all honesty, it was a short drive and not too bad a stretch of road, but I was still afraid. It's just a fact about me. So she was happy I had come, and I was happy I had found the courage, and we enjoyed a nice visit.

I realized that I gave a sigh of relief as I took my exit off the freeway after the drive back toward my house. I made it there and back. No crashes, no tires falling off (I always seem to worry about that when driving high speeds), no encounters with road rage or random shootings, which were not uncommon in our city. No problems had befallen me, so I was feeling relieved and more relaxed as I slowed down on the off-ramp.

The exit I took arrives at a very busy intersection in a major shopping area. There are many lanes of traffic in all four directions. I sat at a red light in one of the left-hand-turn lanes, planning to then head east toward home. I knew it would be a long light, and I just sat waiting, still marveling that I had actually made the trip safe and sound.

Suddenly, off to my left, beyond the lanes to my side, I noticed a man in a wheelchair. A man sitting alone in a wheelchair in a fairly large dirt area near some bushes, on a dirt corner sloping down from the freeway and sort of perpendicular to the lanes of traffic. He was holding a cardboard sign, which seemed insignificant to me at that moment. All I could think was, "How did he get there?" A homeless man, alone, in a wheelchair, on a slopping dirt hill, on the corner of a very busy intersection, with seemingly no way to get to that spot. I could not imagine how he had gotten there, unless crossing heavy traffic. Even then, he'd have to maneuver his chair up that dusty dirt slope. How did he do it? Had he had help? Still stuck at the red light, I observed the man. The sign he held showed he was asking for help, food, or money, or what exactly I can't remember.

It was his face that struck me. His expression. His expression is what I remember. It wasn't what I normally saw on the faces of those I had seen on street corners holding signs and begging. I had seen sadness and desperation or, more commonly, a lack of expression, but this man was different. He had a look of shame on his face. Shame. His look of shame struck me so strongly that my heart began to pound, and I wanted to help him. I wanted to give him the few dollars in my purse. It struck me so strongly I wanted to go to him. I looked around at the lanes of traffic separating me from him. How could I go to him, or even hand him any money? I felt a surge of desperation. How could I get to him? I couldn't. I couldn't leave my car. I couldn't drive close enough to him. I knew the light was about to change. I could not reach him, nor could he reach me if I were to offer some cash out the window. My heart pounded more. Time was running out. I kept thinking, "Why is he ashamed? How did he get there? And why did he choose such an inaccessible spot?"

The light turned green, and I had no choice but to move on. As I turned, I glanced back. His face and situation tugged at me. I looked for a way to reach him. I saw none. I could not reach him, and I drove on.

He seemed to have such need, and how would he get help there in that spot? His face haunted me. Why did he feel shame? I suppose any one of us in his position, forced to beg alone on a roadside, might feel shame. I wondered how he had gotten in this situation. He was disabled. What illness or injury had befallen him? What pain had he endured? Was his situation brought on by poor choices, or had life dealt him a bad hand of hurtful and painful circumstances through no choice of his own? I started to cry. A voice had said to help him, but I did not. I couldn't. I cried. I cried because he felt shame. I cried because I had failed to help him. I felt shame. I cried all the way home.

I was suddenly reminded of a day many years earlier. I was nineteen or twenty years old and riding my bike in my neighborhood. As I cycled down a road at the edge of the housing tract with homes on one side and an open field on the other side, I was enjoying the massaging, warm sunshine and the energizing breeze in my face. I suddenly noticed a young girl my age or a bit younger walking toward me on the other side of the street. Something about her was "off." Something was wrong. As we got closer to each other and we passed, I saw she was crying. I got that same pull in my gut that I had experienced this day for the man on the corner. My heart went out to that girl. I wondered what was wrong. I wondered if I should ask her, or would I be intruding? I kept riding, but something very similar to a sense of guilt gnawed at me. I decided to turn and ride back to her. As I turned, she was nowhere in sight. I looked and looked, but she was gone. Had she entered one of the houses that might be her home? I suddenly thought of the Bible verses that say we sometimes unawarely entertain angels. I felt guilty. I hadn't "entertained" this girl. Did she really need help? Had it been a test that I had failed? I passed her by with no offer of sympathy or help. I rode home wondering if she were "real" or an angel sent to test my concern for others. Whatever the case, I felt I had failed. After all these many years, I had never forgotten that day.

So here I was, confronted with another who needed help, and it tugged at my heart. I wanted to help immediately but found no way to do so. Though I had wanted to help, in the end, I had still done nothing. I felt upset. So here I was, crying. I cried for the man on the corner. I cried for my failure. I cried for his shame and mine.

I thought of this man for days, weeks actually. A few times, I tried to tell the story of seeing him and would cry again. I wondered what I was to do or learn. I wondered if God was asking me to become involved with the homeless somehow. My husband and I were already helping indirectly by giving contributions to the local shelter, but it seemed so impersonal. It didn't feel like much.

I decided to take the tour that the local shelter offered and maybe become involved with helping the homeless. It was three and a half hours long, I was told, and would cover every area, including the men's shelter, women's shelter, families' shelter, and children's shelter. That sounded good, I thought. Maybe a particular area would stand out and draw my interest. That didn't happen. I purposefully tried to remain open to any tugging at my heart, but nothing called to me. The closest thing I felt to a pull at all was the need for blankets in the men's shelter. I had become a knitter and also did some crochet and had already made prayer shawls and some blankets. I figured I could make some to donate to the shelter. I spent the time finding out what was needed in each area, but nothing spoke to me. I never did volunteer or work there in any way. I did learn a lot about what was being offered in our community.

In the end, after many weeks and months, I decided that the lesson was that we stay aware of people around us, people who may be in need, and to help when we can or are called to do so. If the only way to help is to pray, then we pray. I had prayed for the man on the corner. I prayed for him while I cried because I knew nothing else to do, and I had prayed for him since. I wondered about him. Again, I wondered if he was a human being or an angel sent to test me. One thing I have learned is that God does not always require us, in the end, to actually follow through with what he originally asked. Sometimes, he wants to find out if we are willing to obey him and will say yes even when we do not want to. At least that has been true for me. It was that way for Abraham when he was willing to sacrifice his own son, Isaac, when God asked him to yet, in the end, was not required to do so. That story has always amazed me. In my life, God has sometimes asked me to do a thing I really did not want to do. After struggling yet deciding to say yes, it has, more than a few times, turned out the need was no longer there or my service was no longer needed. We never know when that might be the case, but we can know that it is always to our benefit to say yes to God. God doesn't always need our help, but he wants our willingness.

The man in the wheelchair on that particular corner remains a mystery to me. How did he get there? How had he ended up in his situation? Was the expression on his face shame, as it so strongly struck me? Why did he feel ashamed? Why did I feel such a call to help him when I couldn't? I do know that I had been willing. It seems his being in my path that day was for some reason. I'm not certain what that reason is, but if nothing else, it is a reminder to me that there are many who are not as fortunate as I; and I or any one of us, for varying reasons, could find ourselves in his shoes one day. In many ways, we are all just a step away from ruin. One single bad choice or one single accident or illness could land us in a wheelchair, possibly sitting on a dusty dirt corner, holding a sign, begging for help from strangers passing by. We really do not know what we might do when faced with desperation.

I will probably never see that man again. I may never see that corner again. We have since moved five states away from where we were living. In our current city, I have not yet encountered a beggar on the street. Still, there will always be those in need. It's my duty to pay attention, be aware, and be sensitive enough to notice those whom I may be able to help. I know it could just as easily be me in need. Someone's kind word or help can mean everything to one who is hurting or lonely. It doesn't matter the reason for their situation so much as it does our willingness to be used by God for his purpose—to love one another. Anyone of us could be the man on the corner. Maybe his being there that day and my notice of him was simply for me to take note and to tell this story.

The Dream

Sometimes, the most ordinary of days or events end up being very poignant. Common daily activities can become deeply imbedded in our soul and psyche, and may even be life changing. It isn't always noticed or recognized at the time, but in retrospect, the ordinary can be anything but ordinary.

When I was growing up, life was good and fun, from my prospective. I have memories of feeling safe and carefree. Childhood fears existed but were minimal. I have childhood memories as far back as three and four years of age and many very definite memories beginning at age five. My only brother was born in Illinois. I came along a little over three years later, born in Ohio. My two younger sisters came three and four years later in Alabama. By the time we lived in Georgia, where my dad had a private pediatric practice, I was five years old, and I attended a kindergarten in our church.

I remember much from Georgia. I remember our house, our yards, and street—a dirt road. I remember our neighbors, one house on either side of ours. Our home was red—painted brick, I think. I remember the creek across our road where we waded. I remember zillions of summertime fireflies—lightening bugs, we called them. I remember making mud pies, trying to make a small swimming pool, on a hot summer day, out of a plastic sheet and boards with my little neighbor friend. I remember chasing the ice cream truck with my brother and buying an ice cream sandwich for a nickel, given to us by our mother. I remember my brother falling from a tree and getting the wind knocked out of him and how I worried he was hurt. I remember our little kitty named Flea Bag getting crushed between a car tire and the carport wall as he got in the way of my dad pulling in. I remember trying to learn to ride a bike on that dusty dirt road, using a neighbor's bike that was much too big for me. I remember the kumquat bushes. I remember hiding under a table in my dad's office when I didn't want a shot I had to be given. I remember our church and special Easter outfits my mom made for all of us. I remember running head on into a boy on the kindergarten playground and having my first loose tooth knocked even looser. It went down the drain as my teacher washed my bloody mouth and tried to soothe me while I cried. I remember much more, and that is covering only age five.

We then moved to Kentucky. My dad was being called into the ministry, and he left his pediatric practice to attend seminary in Louisville. He and my mom packed us up, and off we went to our new home. Instead of three years of schooling, my dad ended up completing seven before moving us to California, where he became the Old Testament and archaeology professor at Golden Gate Baptist Theological Seminary in Mill Valley, across the Golden Gate bridge north of San Francisco. We lived in San Rafael, a little farther north still and in Marin County. Of course, I have a ton of memories of the California years, spanning eighth grade through high school and one year of college before I moved away to another part of California. But it is the years in Kentucky—grades one through seven—that have made the biggest impression on me and hold my fondest memories. When I think of childhood, I think of Louisville, Kentucky—our home, our neighborhood, our church, our schools, our friends galore, and the changing seasons. All these hold special and precious memories for me. It was also when I first started writing letters, something I have enjoyed to this day. I wrote to the friend I left in Georgia, and I wrote to my grandpa. I remember three- and five-cent stamps. I remember walking to the mailbox and the wonder of how my letters got from there into the hands of those to whom I wrote.

Spring, summer, autumn, and winter were so different, each with its particular feel to the air and excitement of that season. Spring brought the winter thaw, flowers, trees budding, and Easter. There are many Easter memories, such as specially made Easter dresses, church services, Easter baskets, and Easter dinners. Spring also brought my April birthday and the slumber parties I was allowed. My mom and dad always made sure that I and my girlfriends had a good time. One longtime friend remembers my dad's grilled burgers and my mom's cookies and snacks.

Summer brought the end of the school year and many long, lazy days. We spent endless hours involved in a myriad of activities outside. Friends were plentiful; and ideas, endless. Iced tea was a staple and kept us going on those hot days. My bicycle became my constant companion. The miles I rode were full of adventure and too numerous to count. I had a bike to ride even as a young girl, a hand-me-down from my brother once he got a bigger bike, but the beautiful, new, green Schwinn I received on my twelfth birthday is the bike I had the adventures with. It is still with me today. Though a few times, I have considered selling it or giving it away, and though I have another bicycle, I have never been able to part with my green Schwinn. It has been kept in good condition, is still rideable, and is ridden at times. It is too near and dear a friend to part with.

Autumn brought a new school year and all that entails. New clothes, new shoes, school supply shopping. It brought a chill to the air. Leaves turned their many colors and floated to the ground, leaving the trees bare and asleep until spring. Raking those leaves and jumping in the piles we made was a fun activity. Fall brought Halloween with the costumes my mom made and an endless supply of candy after trick or treating. I remember my parents once putting together a Halloween fun house in our basement for their friends.

Thanksgiving came with the delicious turkey dinner and pies. We had the warmth of our heater and the warmth of our family as the days grew colder.

Winter brought the excitement of Christmas, snowy days, and being let out of school early as the roads were soon to be too snowy for the buses to drive us home safely. Some days, we had no school at all. We made snowmen, snow angels, snow balls, and ate snow cones made with real snow and juice. Our Christmas tree and decorations went up. We had homemade advent calendars made by my mother, and we counted down the days as we ate one candy a day until Christmas Day finally arrived. At the age of seven, I received a much-wanted kitten for Christmas. She was loved and adored by the entire family for many years until she died at age twenty-three. I remember the day my mom called to tell me Calico had died. I was thirty, married, had three children, and cats and dogs as well as other pets. I accepted the news bravely and then promptly bawled my eyes out upon hanging up the phone. An important part of my childhood and history was gone.

The uncountable and endless memories I have cannot all be told here. What I have told is only the tip of the iceberg, a tiny portion of a giant catalog stored in the vast warehouse of my memory banks. Most of them are good; some of them sad or of fears, but all of great value.

During those years in Kentucky, when my dad was in school, he was also working part time for the Kentucky Commission for Handicapped Children, keeping his pediatric skills up and earning family income. He did part-time pediatric work for many years, even after our move to California. I remember at least one occasion when I went with my dad to the hospital. It was a Saturday. My mom packed us both a sack lunch, and off I went to work with my dad. I remember he made rounds, and I remember seeing at least one sick child along with him. We ate our lunch together in what I assume was the doctor's lounge. It was a special day and a glimpse into my dad's life. I was fortunate because both my dad and my brother let me tag along with them. My brother and his friends were quite interesting to me, and I found my dad interesting too. I liked being with both of them. Dad was pretty busy between school and his jobs, but I have bountiful memories of him spending time with me in one way or another. Some of these times included bike rides while I rode that green Schwinn. One of the last times that Schwinn was ridden was when Dad came to visit not too many years ago. He rode it while I rode another.

On Saturdays, my dad went to our church and set up Sunday school rooms for the following morning classes. He was minister of education at the church during the last two years we were in Louisville, and preparing the classrooms was a job he did every week. I tagged along. I helped arrange chairs, clean blackboards, and put new chalk in the trays. The church was a three-story building, if I remember correctly, and I followed my dad around, upstairs and downstairs, into all the rooms that needed prepared. I especially took pride in setting up the classrooms where my age group met. I knew I was making it nice for myself, my classmates, and my teachers. It was this Saturday activity with my dad that led to a recurring dream that became significant in my life. All of these childhood experiences were significant and shaped my life, but this particular activity became especially important and used in an especially significant way.

I was barely thirteen years old. I relied heavily on my parents, as any child does. My safety and well-being were in my home where adults were in charge. I had my dad, my mom, and my aunt too, who lived with us. The many activities we all did as a family made a huge impression on me. The fact that my parents took us to church for worship and Bible study was no small influence.

So the dream. Literally a dream while I slept. I dreamed I was following my dad all over the church, up and down the stairs, to prepare all the teaching rooms, just as I did with him in reality. As we would approach a staircase to descend, he would suddenly go out of my sight, and my eyes would close and all would go dark. I tried and tried, but I couldn't open my eyes, and I would stumble on the stairs trying in desperation to see my dad and catch up to him. I would panic and struggle to see, but I couldn't and he was gone, way ahead of me. I didn't scream. I just kept trying to open my eyes, maneuver the stairs, and find my dad. No matter how hard I tried, I was lost in the dark, alone on the stairs, afraid. Suddenly, a face would pop out of the darkness and jeer at me. It was the face of a boy I knew and found difficult to like. He would laugh at me and frighten me further. My panic would rise as I tried to get away from this boy and catch up to my dad, but still my eyes would not open. The only thing I could see at all was the jeering face of the frightening boy. I kept moving forward down the stairs stumbling in the dark and beginning to cry when I would then awake with the words in my mind, "I'm lost without my father. I'm lost without my father." At first, it was simply a nightmare where I was afraid because I couldn't find my dad in the dark. Literally, I was lost on the stairs, in the dark, without my dad.

I dreamed this dream again, then again, and again. Quite a few times, this scenario met me in my sleep. I was regularly attending Sunday school and worship services. I don't remember a single sermon, but I do remember beautiful music from the piano and beautiful singing from the music director. I heard the words to the songs he sang. I didn't know it at first, but I came to realize later that the Holy Spirit was working on me and calling me to God. Each time I had the dream, I would awake saying, "I'm lost without my father. I'm lost without my father." After a little while, the dream took on more than just a literal meaning. I began to realize that I was lost without my Heavenly Father. I was lost without God. My closed eyes were eyes that did not yet know the truth of God's love. The jeering face came to represent Satan, who would prefer me to stay lost and afraid. As this dream worked on my spirit, I would awaken repeating, "I'm lost without my Heavenly Father. I'm lost without my Heavenly Father." I came to know that as a fact.

As is common in Southern Baptist Churches, where we attended, there was an altar call at the end of each service. Those with special needs or those wanting to join the church or those wanting to make a public profession of faith in Jesus Christ could walk forward and talk to the pastor while a hymn was being sung. I'll never forget the Sunday night I went forward at the end of the service. The old familiar hymn "Just as I Am" was being sung. God was talking to me. He was telling me to come to him and know him and love him and follow him. I heard his voice as the Holy Spirit worked on me. I got hot and sweaty. I felt all eyes were looking at me. I hesitated. I was afraid to walk up to the pastor. I was only thirteen, and I didn't understand it all, but I knew I had to go. I had to answer God yes or no, and I wanted to say yes. By the time the third verse was being sung, "Just as I am though tossed about, with many a conflict, many a doubt," I knew those words were for me. I needed to answer God's calling, even if I didn't know yet all that it would entail. I did know I was "lost without my Father" and God wanted me just as I was. I walked forward to the pastor as the congregation kept singing. God called me to him, and I went to him. I acknowledged and accepted God and his son Jesus Christ who was sent to earth and who died for my sins to save me and give me eternal life. I gave him my heart and life. Even at that age, I knew my life was now different, and it had changed forever.

That evening, my dad questioned me some to make sure I understood my decision. I did understand. Not too many weeks later, I was baptized in the church by my dad rather than by the pastor. I and another girl about my age were baptized the same Sunday. I didn't share my dream with him, and I never shared it at all with anyone until many years later and now in this writing. I don't know why. It was a true and real decision and was my first encounter with God personally. First, he spoke through the dream, and then he spoke to me during "Just as I Am." I knew it was God speaking to me, and we've been on speaking terms ever since.

The first instruction God gave me after the call was to go apologize to a neighbor friend. We had had a fight, an actual "rolling on the floor, hitting each other" fight. It occurred at my house. I lost patience with her and lost my temper. My mother broke it up and sent her home and then had words for me. I no longer remember what the fight was about, and my friend doesn't remember it at all. I do, and I felt guilty about it then. God let me know I needed to ask her forgiveness and make things right. I did. I remember talking to her while we stood in the driveway between two houses. She forgave me easily, and forty-five years later, living thousands of miles apart, shortly after that time and ever since, we have remained friends who love and support each other. That is evidence of God's restorative power. She became another whom I wrote frequently, and she wrote back. We continue to write to each other.

Many days and years have passed since those childhood days when God first spoke to me. He used the dream based on an activity with my earthly father to reach me and call me to know him, my Heavenly Father. God has spoken to me many, many times since then. Sometimes, he has spoken to me through a person; sometimes, he has spoken to me through books, the Bible, a sermon, a song, an event, a pet, or nature. Most often, I hear his whisperings in the quiet of my mind. I have sometimes been quick to hear and listen and sometimes slow or failed to hear him altogether. In my growing-up years, I had every opportunity to come to know God. He used my parents and the church to reach me. He first spoke to me in the dream. He speaks to me still. I only have to be still and listen. He is there. He listens to me, and I listen for his responses however he chooses to answer and in whatever way. Even in a dream.

Auntie Bill

As far back as I can remember, my Aunt Beulah, known as Auntie Bill to me and my siblings, was always there. As far back as age three, I can remember her presence; and by age five and beyond, the memories of her in my everyday life are numerous. She lived with us for the majority of my growing-up years in Kentucky. Both before and after the Kentucky years, she lived nearby and was very often in our home. Our home was hers. It wasn't until much later that she went back to her original home in Missouri and stayed there for several years. She then returned to California for her last years. It was my family's treat and mine to have her presence in our lives again.

While growing up in Kentucky, every day, at every meal, at every birthday, at every Christmas, New Year's, Easter, and every special day, vacations, or ordinary days, Auntie Bill was there. She's in many family photos. She lived with us as part of our family. She had a job and went to work; she cooked and baked and cleaned, and stayed with us kids when Mom and Dad had to be away. She helped care for us when we were well or sick and was a part of all we did. She was a very special member of our family. There were no grandparents around or any other family nearby, so Auntie Bill was my only special grown-up who wasn't a parent.

Auntie Bill was fun and funny; and though you didn't always see it, she had a feisty side that I thoroughly enjoyed when it appeared. I felt she was always on my side, but she also would tell me when I was acting "ugly." No matter what, I always had the feeling she was rooting for me and wanted the best for me. My Auntie Bill was quiet but was very caring, generous, giving, thoughtful, and put others first.

Some of my special memories of Auntie Bill are very simple. A vague and very early memory is of us getting ourselves locked inside a train station restroom. I was too young to remember much about it, but my parents and Auntie Bill confirmed that story.

Not being one to drink milk, Auntie Bill used orange juice on her breakfast cereal. As a child, I found that interesting as we sat at the table eating cereal together. I realized later it was not something particular only to her.

As a child, when I was afraid during nighttime thunderstorms, I would call to Auntie Bill, and she would get out of her bed from her bedroom down the hall and come to me, lie down beside me a little while, and comfort me. One night, I had a terrible bloody nose. She came to me when I called then went downstairs after my dad, a doctor, for further help. If I was sick or afraid at night, I could call her, and she would come, never seeming angry or upset.

Sharing the upstairs with my sisters, we shared the upstairs bathroom with her. My Auntie Bill had pretty things in the bathroom that I found interesting, the main one being her bath oil beads. She offered to let me try some for my bath one night. I remember feeling so grown-up using her grown-up lady bath beads. It wasn't more than a few minutes until I realized those bath beads and I didn't get along. The smell of them and feel of the water made me so sick to my stomach that I had to leave the bath. It's a special memory, she sharing her bath beads with me; but to this day, I have never used bath oil beads again. She and I talked about that a few times and laughed.

Another special memory is when I drew her name on one of our Friday family nights. We did many different family things on Friday nights, but one was to draw names then go to Roses dime store and choose a gift for the person whose name we had drawn. The rule was we could spend only a few dollars. I had fun choosing and buying a gift for Auntie Bill and surprising her when we got home, each of us revealing whose name we had drawn and giving the gift we had chosen. She accepted my gift graciously and as if I had so pleased her.

One special memory for me regarding Auntie Bill is of my ninth birthday when she gave me a red leather Bible with my name engraved on the front, and inscribed to me inside in her hand. Though I have acquired other Bibles since then, I still have and use that red leather Bible. I keep it in a prominent place. It is one of the greatest gifts she ever gave me, as well as the gift of herself—her time, her thought, her unconditional love.

When I grew a bit older and Auntie Bill moved into a nearby apartment, I was given her bedroom as my own room. I liked having my own room, but I missed her being there, especially at night. She was still with us very often and for weekends and all the special days, but it did feel odd taking her room at first. I would ride my bicycle to her apartment to visit her, and she always greeted me warmly. Though she rarely showed it, I knew there were things that bothered Auntie Bill at times, but I never ever felt I was a bother to her. Not once. She welcomed me then and welcomed me to her very last days.

When I was thirteen, we moved to Marin County California, just north of San Francisco. After we moved, Auntie Bill followed and then again moved into her own apartment. She lived on the Golden Gate Baptist Seminary campus in Mill Valley, where she held a job as a secretary. I have a special memory, during my high school years, of taking the bus to her apartment after school one Friday and spending the weekend with her. She made grilled cheese sandwiches for dinner that night. No one made grilled cheese sandwiches as well as she did. It was one of her specialties because she liked them so much. They were delicious because she put an extra amount of cheese on them. She gave me her bed to sleep in, and she took the couch—no ifs, ands, or buts. She wanted me to have her bed. It felt special being there with her and her things.

If you were to play Yahtzee with Auntie Bill, watch out! Even in her later years, she would win 99 percent of the time. It was just uncanny, the number of Yahtzees she could roll, even in one game. She did not cheat. She would never cheat. And even in her last years, when any one of us would keep score for her because her hands didn't work so well anymore (as she would explain), she would win. I knew she did not cheat, and that proved it further. She just had this gift, or knack, at winning the game of Yahtzee. We all knew it and experienced it.

I have memories of sitting in the car with Auntie Bill after church on Sundays, both during our Kentucky years and in California years, as we waited for Mom and Dad to be ready to go. We had many conversations about this, that, or another thing and often shared a laugh or a secret over some silly thing. One-on-one, Auntie Bill would talk and tell me what she thought and believed. Those were precious moments. They were snatches of time when I got to know her further.

Something she and I shared was a love of writing and receiving letters. We both enjoyed pretty stationery. When Auntie Bill lived in Missouri, we would write to each other. We started writing each other even more once she was back in California. We lived in different cities and sent letters since we were unable to see each other as often as we would have liked. It became a natural thing to write to her very often, and she would answer every letter until she was no longer able.

I enjoyed receiving her letters and have kept some of them. It made me happy to write to her because I knew she enjoyed receiving letters.

During my visits with Auntie Bill while she was still able, we would sit and do word search puzzles together. I took to making personalized word search puzzles for her for a while and would mail them to her. When visiting, I would do her nightly exercises along with her. One night, we played "Simon Says" and made up exercises to do and copy each other until she tired. Auntie Bill enjoyed watching the game show *Family Feud*, as did I, so we would watch the show together and throw out answers to the questions given by the show host.

You might have known my Auntie Bill as a very quiet person, but there was a lot behind that quiet demeanor. Auntie Bill was full of fun and some mischief and enjoyed pranks we played on her. She told us many stories of her youth, such as the day a butterfly lighted on her hair and went to school with her or the time her mother sent her to a neighbor's house to ask to borrow a cup of sugar. She was so afraid of their dog that she never did get to the door to ask to borrow the sugar. She told her mother the neighbor didn't have any. With some embarrassment, she would always end that story, saying, "Wasn't that awful of me?" with a frown on her face. She told the story of one of her brothers chasing her out of the house and stubbing her bare toe on a rock, breaking her toe.

She told of her mother's beautiful flowers and how she eventually began growing flowers herself. She said her flowers, though pretty, were never as beautiful as her mother's. She liked to tell the story of parading her baby brother, my father, around for all the neighbors to see, showing him off "because he was such a pretty baby." She was an older sister, and he the youngest of the siblings. I like to think it was her early devotion to him and their early bonding, which kept them close and devoted to each other throughout the years.

Auntie Bill was quiet, but she was a strong person, able to endure discomforts and hardships. She was very tolerant, fun, patient, kind, and very generous. She was content to be behind the scenes. She'd give you or do for you anything she thought you needed or would make you happy. Auntie Bill was different than many in that she never learned to roller skate, ride a bike, or drive a car. She never married, and she never gave birth to a child. She lived simply and quietly, yet richly, and she enriched my life and the lives of others.

When Auntie Bill was quite elderly yet still able to attend her church worship services along with my father, with whom she lived, one of her greatest joys was receiving a gentle kiss on the cheek from her pastor as she left the sanctuary. I will never forget the first time she told me about his special attention. She was so surprised and so happy. She liked her pastor. She found him to be a nice man and a handsome man and enjoyed the attention. She would continue to mention it to me each Sunday when I would call and talk with her and my dad. It was such a gift her pastor gave her, to pay attention to her in that way each week. It made Auntie Bill feel special and so happy that in turn made me very happy. It seemed so significant to her that I let him know, more than once, what a gift he was giving her. When Auntie Bill was no longer able to live at home or to attend services, her pastor continued to pay attention to her by visiting her in the convalescent home where she lived the remainder of her life. Being the person she was, Auntie Bill became a special resident to those who cared for her, and she continued to receive care and attention from her church family. It was a precious gift they gave her.

There were some things my Auntie Bill very much loved and enjoyed. She loved flowers, especially pansies. She enjoyed watching birds and particularly liked Cardinals. She liked butterflies, loved cats, enjoyed a good grilled cheese sandwich, and enjoyed sunny days. She did *not* like rainy days. She enjoyed her pastor's care and attention. She loved me. She loved us all until her last day.

On November 29, 2012, at the age of ninety-four, our very special Auntie Bill left this world to be with God. He gave her to us for many years; and though we all hated for her to leave, we were happy she was free of old age and illness and was in eternity with our Heavenly Father.

The Silver Tree

Red, yellow, blue, green, red, yellow, blue, green… Slowly the color wheel turned, casting one color after another on the branches of our Christmas tree. It was an aluminum silver Pom Pom tree. Red, yellow, blue, green… My father, mother, aunt, brother, two sisters, and I stood at the edge of our front yard, by the street, and admired our just decorated, shining Christmas tree. It stood in our front window, one of many trees decorating our neighborhood during the Christmas season.

We stood in the cold and snow and quiet hushed sounds that a snow-covered world brings. I can remember knowing it had snowed during the night, before I opened my eyes upon waking in the morning because sounds were different. They were muted and hushed. So there my family stood in the quiet winter night of the Christmas season and watched the tree change colors.

To further add to the snowy, wintery experience, my mother added spray-on snow to the corners of each little window pane that made up the large front window. As the colors shined on the tree, one after the other—red, yellow, blue, green—each of us told which color we liked best. It was difficult to choose with each color giving the tree a momentary different personality. I chose the blue as my favorite. It seemed to match the chilliness of the winter night and the mystery of Christmas time.

We decorated our Christmas tree together as a family. The silver Pom Pom tree didn't require much putting together or decorating. My brother, sisters, and I were each given an equal number of branches to insert into the holes on the trunk. The trunk was a wooden pole, painted silver, with carefully designed drilled holes to hold the pom pom branches at just the right angles to shape a tree. Once the pom pom branches were in, we all placed the shiny red ball ornaments that my mother had unpacked, on the tree. A few years we tried other colors of balls, but red was the favorite. Only red, and only those ornaments. Nothing else was placed on the tree. Nothing else was needed. Once the red balls were all evenly in place around the tree, the color wheel was turned on and placed in the best position to illuminate the silver branches. Red yellow, blue, green—the wheel turned slowly. It was mesmerizing to sit in the dark and watch the tree as it reflected back the colors in turn. Red, yellow, blue, green. The red light drowned out the red balls to some degree, but it was a vibrant Christmas color. The yellow was the brightest and cast a warm glow. The green was another Christmas color and seemed cheery with life. The blue, however, held that mystery to it. It was more subdued, cooler, faint, and cast the color of a black sky with stars that seemed to twinkle a faint blue. There was crispness to the blue color along with a calm and quietness that was relaxing. It was peaceful. The blue reminded me of what it might have looked and felt like the first Christmas—the night Jesus was born. The night sky might have been dark blue/black with bluish twinkling stars. The night calm and quiet when then the angels appeared to shepherds. In the traditional Christmas story, I picture a calm, serene nativity on a winter night. The blue light cast on our silver tree reminded me of what that night might have been like and the mystery and meaning of Jesus' birth, as told to us in the Bible.

My family didn't always use the silver Pom Pom tree; but we did for a few years in the mid-sixties, when they became popular for a while. Other years, we had green trees, either buying a cut tree or going to a tree farm and cutting one down. At the tree farms, we each had a turn at sawing the trunk of the tree till it came down. Our Christmas tree was a family affair no matter what kind of tree we used.

Of all the Christmas trees we had, the silver Pom Pom stands out in my mind. Looking at the tree as the colors shown red, yellow, blue, green while standing in the yard at night has special memories for me. Some years ago, my father gave me the silver Pom Pom tree and two color wheels to go with it. We put the tree up that year and let our children enjoy it. They and their friends and many of our friends had never seen such a Christmas tree. I showed it to my piano students at the time. It was new to them too. We got a lot of enjoyment out of the tree and sharing it with others.

Some would say that a silver tree is too artificial and too modern to use for Christmas. I can understand that thinking. It certainly isn't like a live green tree. It has no fragrance of pine. There is a charm and appeal to me in a green tree decorated in an old-fashioned way with strung popcorn, colorful construction paper chains, cranberries, and bows. I enjoy that type of tree. But I have to admit that the shining silver Pom Pom tree with the rotating color wheel casting red, yellow, blue, green shades on the silver branches holds a mystery and special memories. I like shiny sparkling things. The expressions of the silver tree, as the colors change, still captivate me.

After much use, both color wheels have stopped working. The motors have burned out after turning the wheels thousands and thousands of times. For a few years, we have had no color wheel, though I have now found some available for purchase and plan to buy one. Even without a color wheel, the silver Pom Pom tree went up in our house this past Christmas. We put the old familiar red shiny balls from my childhood on it. As I put the tree together one afternoon, placing the branches in the perfectly drilled holes in the silver trunk, I remembered years past when my family put the tree up together. I knew my parents and siblings had all touched the branches. As I placed the red balls on the branches, I knew they had been handled by all in my family. I wondered if any of their fingerprints still remained on them. There is a part of my mother, father, aunt, brother, and sisters in that tree. I remembered our home at the time we used the silver tree. I remembered the yard we stood in and how the tree shone brightly in our window for all passersby to see. I remember our neighborhood lit up with other trees in windows as we all waited for Christmas Day. I still remember those winters, the cold air, the silence of a snowy night. I remember watching the colors perform their miracles on the tree and how the blue seemed so calming, so enchanting, so chilly, and so mysterious— how it reminded me of what that first Christmas night might have been like and what Christmas is about.

It doesn't matter what kind of Christmas tree we choose in decorating our home to celebrate the season. What matters is that we celebrate Jesus' birth and God's gift to us. The silver Pom Pom tree does that for me and also holds special memories of years past.

Smokey

I entered the animal shelter and wondered if I should even be there. If you are an animal lover, as I am, you know how dangerous it can be to enter a shelter. You are very likely to bring home yet another pet. I did purposefully go to the shelter even though we already had several cats and dogs and other smaller animals as part of our menagerie. Yet my daughter's special cat, Muffin, her very own pet, had recently been "put to sleep" due to a deadly tumor making the cat very sick. Muffin had turned out to be quite a wild creature and would rather attack your ankles and bite you than play cutely or snuggle. In reality, he had not turned out to be a very good pet for a little girl. We called him Monster Cat, and the veterinarian even put that name on Muffin's chart after his first dealing with Muffin. I warned him. He found out quickly why the warning.

In that veterinarian's office, Muffin was forever tagged Monster Cat. Muffin was mean and unpredictable. So here I was at the animal shelter in hopes of finding a gentle, sweet, playful, loving, fuzzy, cute kitten for my young daughter.

I entered the room that housed the cats. It was a small shelter and had a small cat room. As I turned the corner, I immediately saw and heard a tiny, gray kitten—a very tiny kitten, too small to be away from his mother. Tiny as he was, he let out a screech and holler way too big for such a small body. The fuzzy little gray kitten went berserk and howled and lunged and actually frightened me a little. He screamed! I wondered what was wrong with this poor little kitten that he could call out so deafeningly. I stood and stared at him and tried to quiet him, but he wasn't easily quieted. He was upset and howling, but very cute as kittens can be. He obviously needed a mother. There he was, a baby all alone in a metal cage at a sterile shelter, just too little to be alone. My heart strings were definitely being pulled in just those few minutes with that fuzz ball of a kitten. I was hesitant, though, to take him home. His behavior was disconcerting. I wanted a sweet, cuddly cat for my daughter, not a maniac. We had just had one of those.

I left the shelter feeling relieved that I hadn't too hastily adopted another pet, yet I felt uneasy about leaving the kitten alone in that sterile cage. He needed a home and a mother, even if a human one. I wasn't so sure it should be me; but all the rest of that day, and especially that night, I couldn't get the tiny screeching animal out of my head. I wondered how he was as I pictured him in the cold metal cage alone. I mentally went through all the reasons why I should not adopt him. I had just as many reasons why I should, and my heart hurt knowing I had left him alone in his predicament when he had so loudly made his plight known. There was something about him that called to me. I didn't realize it then, but I needed that kitten as much as he needed me. By morning, I knew I was going back to the shelter.

I got my three children and my husband off to school and work and took off myself for the shelter. I had not told anyone I was going. I felt I needed to hurry. I was worried about the gray kitten. I wondered if he would still be there. If he was, I knew I would be bringing him home. I had a small carrier with me. I had learned long ago not to try to drive a car with a cat running loose. Most cats don't handle car rides well, and I doubted this frenzied cat would either. I already had everything a kitten needed. I also had both time and love to give the lonely abandoned creature—one of God's precious creations. I wondered what the kitten's story was and planned to ask. I thought about a name for the baby feline. I kept telling myself he would be for my daughter; but as it would turn out, he was for me.

I entered the shelter, said hello to the same employees who had been there the day before, and hurried to the cat room. I was greeted again by loud screeching and wailing from the tiny gray kitten. He acted wild and crazy just as he had the day before, and screamed at me. All I heard from him was, "Please save me." I looked into his eyes and said, "You are coming home with me."

I asked the workers in the office about him. He had been found alone out along a country road, probably one of many in an unwanted litter who had been dumped and left to die or survive on their own. He was about six weeks old. I said I'd take him. I filled out the necessary papers, paid the fee, and gathered the info needed for future shots the kitten would need. I placed him in the carrier I had brought and took him to the car. He screeched and wailed and flung himself around the entire ride home. I stopped once to check on him, wondering what was wrong with him. His behavior was disturbing, but he seemed physically okay. I decided he was probably traumatized and terrified. I wondered if my decision to adopt him was a good one, or if he would be a problem pet? But he was just so little and young and alone with no mama cat and no siblings. He needed a home and someone to love him. I was game. I needed to love him.

We arrived home. I carried the kitten in and began to settle him into his new home. The house was quiet, and he could explore without commotion. The dogs were outside. They were used to cats, but this kitten was probably not used to dogs. I showed him the litter box and showed him his personal food and water dishes and gave him some food. He chowed down hungrily. I held him and stroked him and spent time with him. I thought about a name. Though it wasn't very original, Smokey seemed an appropriate name for him. I decided I had better wait and introduce him to my family and get their input, especially from my daughter since the kitten was supposed to be for her. However, she didn't know I had gone after this kitten, and I knew that Smokey and I were already falling in love. What *was* it about this little cat that drew me to him, and he to me? As I went about the house, I noticed him following me. If I stayed in one place very long, he settled in nearby to snooze or came to snuggle. He explored, napped, and played a little too. He was already acting more like how a kitten usually acts, and he had quieted down. He did not scream or wail ever again as he had at the shelter. The kids arrived home, and of course, they were interested in the kitten. They played with him and pet him. We all agreed his name would be Smokey.

In theory, Smokey belonged to my daughter; yet in reality, Smokey was mine. We all knew it. Something between that cat and I clicked, and we connected strongly. I mothered him and lavished him with love, and he clung to me. I felt a bit lonely at that particular time—something I kept private. Having that little creature right by me every time I turned around was comforting. One day, I had gone out to my small piano studio, which was a room converted from half of our garage. I entered through the garage; students entered through a separate outside entrance. I used the room not only to teach private piano lessons but also to play piano myself and to practice singing. I wasn't in there very long when I turned on my piano bench and saw Smokey contentedly sleeping on a nearby chair. It struck me then that he was my constant companion quietly shadowing me, wanting to be near. It seemed to give him comfort to be nearby me at all times. It made me feel good and comforted to have him near. Stroking his soft, fuzzy, gray fur gave us both pleasure, and he quietly purred. Smokey and I enjoyed each other's company and found a pal in each other. I let him lay near me or on me everywhere I was. I was sewing quite a bit at the time, and Smokey would nestle in my lap as I sewed. He was just always there, quietly being a friend, loving me in all the ways a cat can show and accepting all the love and attention I gave him.

It wasn't long before I noticed Smokey seemed a little too sleepy and quiet. He seemed lethargic to me, not playing as much as one would expect a young kitten to. He didn't seem to be growing as much as expected either. I wondered if it was my imagination, but his little body felt warm, too warm, as if he might have a fever. Something about him didn't seem quite right. I'd had many cats, and Smokey seemed ill to me. I called our veterinarian friend who lived in our neighborhood and was invited to bring Smokey over, and he'd take a look at him. Smokey did have some fever. Our friend looked him over and said the kitten may just have a cold that would clear up, but I should watch him awhile and see if he improved or not. I did keep an eye on Smokey. He continued to be smaller than the norm and stayed lethargic. He also continued to stick by my side, always pouring out love freely and receiving it back appreciatively.

One day, I decided Smokey needed further examining. Our veterinarian friend picked Smokey up on his way to work one morning and agreed to look him over thoroughly and run tests. He promised to call me in a few hours. Off little Smokey went with a stranger, to another cold sterile cage, but to a place where animals were loved and cared for. I did trust our friend with him. It was a warm spring day the day when Smokey took off to the animal hospital. I was outside, painting some shelves for my daughter's bedroom when I got the call. Our friend informed me that Smokey was very sick and very contagious. He had a serious and deadly cat disease. Just which disease, I no longer remember. Smokey had probably caught it out in the wild before I ever brought him home. Our highly trained and skilled animal doctor friend told me Smokey needed to be euthanized. The news hit me hard. Smokey, put to sleep, forever. My little feline friend and companion was going to die one way or another, and soon. I was told it was important to "put him down" before he became sicklier and before he infected other cats. He gently asked me if I'd like him to inject Smokey at his office and take care of his body or have him bring Smokey home and do the injection in our home with me a part of it. I wanted Smokey home. He said he'd come soon.

I put away the paint, grabbed a shovel, and chose a special spot for Smokey's grave. With each shovel full of dirt, I cried knowing I was losing my special friend that very day, my little friend of only six and a half months, my little friend who offered so much and gave me so much comfort, my little kitten friend who called my help and made me feel special and loved, my little fuzzy friend who accepted all I had to give him. No one was home, nor would anyone be home for hours. It was appropriate. The whole family would not have to watch Smokey die. It was a relationship that only I and the kitten shared, which was about to end so abruptly. It was appropriate that he and I experience his death alone together. I dug the grave as deep as I could, leaving my tears on the dirt that would cover Smokey's body and left it for later. I had a piano student arriving. Fortunately, the student was a good friend, also an animal lover, and would understand my sadness over Smokey's fate.

I started the lesson, but before we were very far into it, the veterinarian arrived with Smokey. I excused myself from the lesson, my student being informed of what must happen, and left her to play on her own and wait if she so chose. I met the doctor in my kitchen and took Smokey from the carrier. He purred at my touch and rubbed his body against me, showing his happiness at being home. I stroked him and talked to him, knowing these were our last moments together. My little gray kitten, only eight months old and tiny for his age, had to die. He had to humanely die now or suffer a terrible death plus infect other cats. He had no idea these were our last moments, or did he? We were so connected in spirit that maybe he understood somehow that we were saying good-bye to each other as he lavished me with his affection. The doctor got the drug ready to administer; and when I gave the okay, he injected Smokey with the liquid that would end his life while the kitten and I continued to caress each other. I talked softly to Smokey while he purred back at me. Fairly quickly, the drug took effect, and Smokey got quiet and lay down. I continued to pet him, and he continued briefly to purr quietly. I cried and told him I was sorry he was so sick and thanked him for his time as my friend. Soon, his breathing stopped. He was gone.

Being a kind friend, our veterinarian offered to help me bury Smokey. I showed him the prepared grave I had already dug, but he said it was not deep enough. The now-deceased Smokey was still contagious for a while, and the grave needed to be deeper to protect other cats from catching the disease. He took my shovel and dug the grave deeper. It was an act of love and kindness that I will never forget. Then we buried Smokey. It was final. Smokey was gone forever. I was sad. Very sad. Our veterinarian friend left, and I went back to my student who had waited. Since I was not up to continuing her lesson, she went on home. I created a little grave marker for Smokey and later planted some flowers.

My day had to continue despite my grief. If you have ever lost a pet you deeply loved, you know how great the grief can be. I have suffered such grief several times. Some don't take the grief of losing a pet very seriously. Some do. That day, I encountered both types. My day continued; and as evening came, I was at our church for Wednesday night choir practice. I went to the piano to prepare to accompany the choir. I found a small plant with a card. A dear friend who had learned of Smokey's untimely death and understood how it affected me, had bought the gift and placed it on the piano. This was the only person who seemed to fully understand how deeply I was affected by my loss. That too was a gift of love and kindness I will never forget. The plant has long since died, but the memory lives on.

Days passed. Weeks and months passed. Other cats came along as well as other pets. It was some years until I fell hard for another cat who became a beloved pal. I had him many years. It was during those years that, one Christmas, my daughter gave me a book of photos and other things she had put together and titled *Mom*. Inside were many photos of people and things and pets. As I flipped the pages, I was caught off guard by some pictures of that tiny, little gray kitten Smokey. Upon seeing his picture, I unexpectedly burst into tears. There he was, my dear little friend who had so filled a need in me as I had filled one for him. There was that tiny pal with whom I had shared a deep love between human and animal. I was startled at how strongly I reacted to the pictures and the memories. My daughter said, "I didn't mean to make you cry."

I have that special book to this day, still out and available to look through. There, amongst all the pictures of my children and family and other people and things I love, are pictures of my pets and my dear beloved Smokey. At the time of this writing, it's been twenty-two years since his death, but I remember him well and with deep emotion—the tiny, lonely, sickly, gray kitten that needed me and I him. The tears still fall.

A Broken Heart

What do you do with a broken heart? What do you do when your heart is broken; your dreams, shattered? What do you do when your world suddenly changes and grief grabs hold of you so strongly that nothing seems familiar anymore, not even yourself? What do you do when all joy is gone and all looks black or in shades of gray? How do you live with a broken heart? How do you continue when all you knew or believed changed in an instant? How do you carry on in a world that you no longer recognize?

If you have lived very many years at all, you have probably suffered a broken heart in some way. A heart may break for varying reasons, some more painful and lasting than others. A broken heart comes from a great loss. The death of a loved one, such as a spouse, child, parent, sibling, friend, or a pet, can bring great feelings of loss and grief. Great loss can occur without physical death. The ending of a friendship or any meaningful relationship is a death. Betrayal within a relationship is a death as well. Even loss of job or health can bring on feelings of grief. All of these are losses of one sort or another; and in some cases, the grip of grief can leave any one of us devastated and feeling alone and a stranger in our own world, the world we thought we knew. Grief can paralyze us to where we cannot function.

Can a broken heart heal? Maybe. Even in healing, there will be scars—possibly lasting scars. In the literal sense of a broken heart, as in a physical heart attack, some die and some live. Those who live bear the scars in and on their body as a reminder of when their body failed them. Life is not the same after a physical heart attack, not entirely; and certainly, whatever normalcy is regained comes after many days and weeks and months as the body heals and regains strength. The body has to get over the shock and debilitation that the heart attack brought on.

When we are emotionally shattered and suffer what we call a broken heart, at first, there is great shock, especially if the loss is sudden. Everything stops, and the world as we knew it is changed. Life cannot go on as usual. We may be too broken to function well, if at all. We may go through the motions without really being present mentally or emotionally. Our senses fail us. Food becomes tasteless; our sense of smell diminishes; things we saw as beautiful lose their beauty; and things we cared about lose their appeal. Activities we enjoyed no longer bring joy or have meaning. We stop doing them. Days are long, and nights are torture. There is uncertainty around every corner. We feel alone and a stranger in the world, even to ourselves.

No one knows exactly how we might react or feel during great loss and grief. We may lose touch with reality and find it difficult to carry on. We may turn to another for help, a professional or one we feel we can confide in. It may be difficult to turn to another for help. We may be embarrassed or unable to take the steps to ask for help. Or the one we would have turned to might be the source of our grief, having died or betrayed us in some way. We may feel we have no one left to turn to. In some cases, we may not seek help in order to keep painful secrets we don't want others to know. Whatever our loss and grief, there is a road we must travel before we regain balance in our life. There is no way around grief. We must travel through it and the loss and anger that will accompany it then, hopefully, emerge better and stronger for it.

In my own deepest grief, the pain was severe and very private. I felt there was no one to turn to. Disbelief and confusion scrambled my thoughts and filled my days and nights with fear, even terror, and tears that would not cease. I was unsure of my future or how I would cope with the present. My mind raced. My appetite left. Days were long. Nights were fitful. I ceased to engage in activities that normally brought me pleasure and relaxation. I couldn't relax. I couldn't concentrate. My knitting sat unfinished. My piano fell silent. When I tried to read, I knew nothing of what I was reading. I didn't care about things as usual. I just went through my days numbly or fearful, and felt very, very alone. Only a few knew there was anything wrong in my life, and details were not shared.

One thing I did continue were my morning walks. They were a source of comfort, to get away and be alone and have a place to cry unseen. My grief was such that I couldn't, or was unwilling, to share it, and the loneliness of bearing the heavy burden alone only added to my pain. I was alone in a very uncertain world. With no one to share, my grief was excruciating at times. I had no answers and knew no one who could help. No help on earth anyway.

I had no help on earth, but I did have help from God in heaven. When all else is gone, God is there. Who knows us better than God? No one. God our creator knows us. God alone knows us in every way. Even when we have no voice but tears, he hears us and understands our cries. The Holy Spirit interprets our deep aching when we cannot speak and God hears. I was so shook up and so deep in my solitary grief that no words would come when I tried to pray; only deep sobbing came from me. Nothing could have hurt me or destroyed me more than the loss I was bearing. The grief it brought was deeper than any other I had ever experienced. God knew that. God knew me. God knows me. In a previous very painful loss, I had become extremely angry with God. I learned a lesson then that God alone is the one who can help us. Though I threw a tantrum and tried to leave him, he would not leave me. In the end, I called to him for help and healing. Now in this much greater loss, I knew to go to God straight away, and he would help me.

One day at a time, God sustained me as I turned to him. Moment by moment, day after day, week after week, month after month and into a year and more, God sustained me. I cried out to him; and though I was struggling, I felt his presence like no other time. The closer I drew to him, the closer it seemed he drew to me. In all of my heartache, struggling silently alone, God heard, and God said, "Trust me. Trust me and love others. Trust me and love. Love and forgive as I have loved and forgiven you." Day after day, I heard him say, "Trust me." I clung to those whisperings like never before. I started each day afraid but remembered I was to trust God and love others. Every step forward was full of uncertainty, yet I pressed forward, trusting God.

Slowly I began to feel some relief from my broken heart. I had small moments of hope and clung to them. I began to find a new confidence that had nothing to do with my circumstances or those around me, or even those near and dear to me. I found confidence in God's care and faithfulness to me. Slowly I gained some equilibrium. Slowly I gained strength and found new worth. One day, after quite some time, I found myself picking up my knitting again, and my piano lid was open with music on the rack. A new book was by my bedside.

As I began to heal, I realized I was much better off, in many ways, than I had been before my great loss and broken heart. My well-being rested less with others and circumstances in my life and more with God, his love, and his purposes for me. Even so, I realized I would never be the same, nor see things the same way again. Some treasured dreams had died and would never be possible, or at least not the same. You cannot undo life happenings. My life and heart had some scars. Though the deep wounds were slowly healing, the scars would remain. It took a very long time for my wounds to heal. I could feel God slowly putting my heart back together piece by piece like a jigsaw puzzle; but I would have the scars, much like a puzzle has the edge lines in it. Sin, ours or another's, will leave scars on our life, reminders of who we are and where we have been. Reminders of the grief we have borne.

As I healed, I had setbacks. Moments of fear and panic would hit me. I had days I knew Satan was toying with me, telling me lies or planting seeds of fear. I would remember God said, "Trust me," and in Jesus' name, I would command Satan to flee from me, and he did. He had to. When we belong to God and the Holy Spirit lives in us, Satan cannot stay if we shoo him away. I shooed him away as often as necessary, and I did it with confidence.

Still much time passed, and I found my grief would reappear, as did my fear. In this life, we often suffer. I found my experience with profound loss and a broken heart left me more sensitive and vulnerable emotionally. I became less trusting, more cynical. Less open. Yet somehow, at the same time, I could feel a new strength growing within me. My trust in God was stronger and growing deeper. Still, certain things would prick a scab still healing, and I would feel intense emotional pain. Most anything, a song, TV show, or conversation, could leave me freshly stabbed. Certain people or places would renew old feelings of pain. A photo or word, or even a name, could send me plummeting to my emotional death again. I wondered if the hurt would ever leave. I begged God to take it away, and I clung to his promises; and again, I heard his words whispered to me, "Trust me." God was aware of my weakness and vulnerability and sustained me—held me tight—as I learned more and more to lean on him, not anyone or anything, for my security.

Very slowly, I gained new confidence and new strength, and oh so slowly, my pain subsided, but it did subside. I faced each day with a new hope—not because all grief and sadness had disappeared, but because I knew God was with me. And no matter how another treated me and no matter what loss, pain, or grief might meet me in the future, I would be safe in God's love and care. That's all I needed and need. I learned better how to truly forgive, and I realized I had no choice but to forgive because I had been forgiven by God through the death of his son Jesus Christ on the cross. God on earth as Jesus Christ, the cross, and his shed blood was for me just as much as it was for those living at that time. I was and am forgiven, and I must forgive and love and trust God with my life. Forgiveness brings healing.

We are not promised a life with no problems, no pain, no sorrow, no loss, or no grief. Grief can and does change us. It did me. I am not the same person I was before my greatly shattered heart. In some ways, time does heal all wounds, but the scars remain. They are a fact I cannot deny or ignore. I don't think exactly as

I did before. I don't trust as easily as I once did. My expectations are different. I expect less maybe. I do care less about some things. In some ways, I am a little bit numb. Maybe more time is needed for full healing. My desires have changed. I am a changed person in some ways, and I have to accept that, but some of those changes are for the better. There is a saying, "If it doesn't kill you, it will make you stronger." There is truth in that. After a long struggle, I believe I am a stronger person for having survived my broken heart and the intense grief that followed. It is easy and tempting at times to become hard-hearted and uncaring and to run from what might hurt, but that isn't the best way to live or is it the life of peace and joy that God gives when we turn our life over to him and trust him.

As in a physical heart attack, a broken heart can heal. We can emerge stronger and more prepared for future days and the struggles we may encounter. Memories of what broke us will remain along with the scars, but scar tissue is thicker than skin and, in a sense, will protect us. God can use these reminders to draw us to him and to heed the whisperings I heard. "Trust me. Love others. Forgive as I have forgiven you." In so doing, we are better for it.

The Piano

It was Sunday morning, and I was sitting in church with my family. We attended Sunday school and worship services every Sunday at a local church that was fairly large, at least in my memory. I was nine, and it may have seemed larger to me than it actually was. I enjoyed Sunday school for my age group; but at just nine years of age, I found myself getting squirmy during "Big Church." There may have been a service especially for children as many churches have, but my memories are of sitting in the main sanctuary with my family. I enjoyed being with and watching adults. I often wonder if they knew how much I watched them. I guess all children observe the adults around them. It's part of learning.

The sanctuary was filled, it seemed. We sang hymns, and then there was the offering collection and special music of some sort. Often, the choir sang a choral piece, and then the sermon was given by the pastor. This particular Sunday, I remember entertaining myself with a Band-Aid I pulled off some injured part of my body. I often used a pencil from the back of the pew and drew little pictures on the bulletin. Sometimes, I practiced writing my name in cursive. I was in the third grade, and we were learning to write in cursive that year. Sometimes, especially in the winter, I carried a fuzzy little muff with me to church; and in its little coin pocket, I carried small candies or Luden's cough drops and coins for the offering plate and, on that particular day, maybe a spare Band-Aid. I just remember pulling a Band-Aid apart into smaller pieces and sticking them to my skin. Anything to entertain myself and stay quiet, I guess. Above all, we needed to stay quiet. I was sitting next to my mom on that Sunday. She allowed me to play quietly with my various little things. It might have seemed that I was paying no attention at all to what was going on around me, but that was not the case.

I was aware of each part of the service, but the two parts and two people who I was most aware were the music director and the pianist. The music director's name was Mr. Roper, and I liked hearing him sing, especially solos. I don't know if I ever knew the pianist's name, and I don't remember it now. It doesn't matter so much, I guess, because I do remember her piano playing, and I remember that very day thinking, "That is so pretty. I want to do that one day. That is so pretty. I want to play the piano." And I would listen to what I thought were the most beautiful sounds coming out of that piano, and I wondered about the lady playing it. I wanted to do what she did. Little did I know what these thoughts would lead to, nor did I realize that either God planted those seeds of thought in my mind or he heard the thoughts and desires of my heart and thought he would use them. God gives us the desires of our heart if they are in line with his plan for us.

My mother played the piano, but our family did not own one. It was something my mother wished for, and one day her wish came true. My father took the entire family to a piano store, and he and my mother chose a piano. It was a cherry wood spinet, Howard brand, made by Baldwin Piano Company. It was not fancy and not real expensive, but it was a beautiful piano that would belong to us. It was a Saturday, or a summer day, or some "no school" day because I was home when the piano was delivered. I remember my mom and I being excited for its arrival and watching out the front door and standing on the front steps as the big delivery truck came down the street and drove up to our house. My mom had already chosen and cleared the spot for the piano. It was to be placed on a small living room wall right inside the front door and around the corner. The men delivering our piano didn't have to take it very far into the house. It was placed against the wall, and my mom played it. I was ten by then.

I remember hearing my mom playing the piano, many nights, as I fell asleep. She played from a book of Broadway hits and also played hymns we sang at church. Sometimes she sang. I remember listening and thinking, "That's so pretty. I want to do that."

I don't know if it was my idea or my parents', but I started piano lessons sometime later at age eleven, as did one of my younger sisters. We went to our lessons on Tuesday afternoons and each lesson cost $2.25. My teacher's name was Laura Weiss. She seemed to me a very old woman. She had white hair, and she had old things in her house. I still have the books she wrote my weekly practice instructions in. She wrote with a red pencil. She was a fairly patient teacher as I remember; and I learned a lot from her, even participating two years in the National Guild of Piano Players. It was a large program I had to play, and it was also by memory. Performances were judged and graded according to their system. I did well. I was in piano lessons less than two full years, though I did play two years in the guild evaluations. I remember, somewhere in the second year, my mother complained that I didn't practice enough and that there was no sense in continuing lessons and paying for them if I was not practicing. I felt guilty, and it was true I had sloughed off in practicing. But I did like playing piano. It was around that time that my family began to prepare to move across the country from Kentucky, where we were, to California. My lessons stopped, and I never had a lesson again until I was around twenty-one years old.

In our new home in California, our piano sat just inside the front door on a small living room wall, similar to where it had sat in our Kentucky home. My mom played it some. I never had lessons while living there, maybe because lessons were too expensive or maybe because I never asked for more lessons. However, I still wanted to play piano and thought about it often. I would sit down and play from my mother's books best I could. I had learned enough to read through music and teach myself, though slowly at first. I also enjoyed just "noodling" around and creating my own pieces. There is a piece I composed at age sixteen called "Melody," which I still play today.

At nineteen, I married and moved away from home to another city. We lived in a house that had a full basement. In that basement, there was a side room that had a few tools in it; but aside from that small room, there was not one single thing in that basement, except an old upright grand piano. It had once been used in the church next door, where we attended. It just sat there against a cement wall in a large empty room. I had that piano available to me, so one day, I decided to go down and play it. I played "Melody," the song I had composed. I practiced scales, and I played from a hymn book we had. The sound bouncing off the walls of the empty basement was big and satisfying. I learned the hymns "When I Survey the Wondrous Cross" and "What a Friend We Have in Jesus" first, as they were two of the easier hymns. I thought about the pianist in the church we attended, and I also remembered the lady playing the piano when I was nine, and I had that old thought, "I want to do that." I certainly was not skilled enough to be a church pianist but maybe one day. After some time, I sought out piano lessons. I started lessons with a teacher at our local music store and was on my way to learning more about playing piano when, just a few months into the lessons, we realized we would be moving. I quit the lessons. We moved. The piano stayed.

We moved to another city, and we became involved in a church there. Just shortly after we started attending that church, the music director came to me and asked if I would like to have an old upright piano that the church was no longer using. I was shocked. Why would he think to ask me that? To my knowledge, I had not discussed piano playing with him. I said yes to the piano, and a few men came and delivered that piano to our house. Again, I had a piano in my home. I played around on it, playing what I could, and one day, I sought out lessons. By that time, our first son had been born. It was a little trickier taking and affording lessons with a one-year-old. I found a teacher who would come to our home, and I began lessons with him and was gaining some knowledge and making some headway when, before long, I realized child number two was on the way. I was very sick with morning sickness—morning sickness that lasted all day, every day. I was miserable, and I quit lessons. We did not live there long either, and before very many more months, we were relocated yet again to another city. The piano stayed behind.

We started attending church in our new city. We had not been in our home very long when I was home with my two young boys one morning and heard a knock at the door. I answered, and there stood two men from the church. They asked if I would like to use an old upright piano that the church was not using. If so, they would bring it in. I don't need to tell you how shocked I was again. I said yes, and in came the piano. "Amazing," I thought. It *was* amazing! Our first home had a piano sitting alone in the basement, discarded when the church we attended had gotten a new one. Our second home had been graced with a piano the church music director told me they were not using. Now, our third home had a piano sitting in it, also given by our church for my use. My mind flashed on my nine-year-old and lifelong wishes of playing the piano one day and my secret desire of playing for church worship services. I stood there and said. "Lord, are you telling me you want me to play the piano?" It occurred to me that I may be a slow learner, and maybe he had been trying to tell me this all along, giving me the opportunity to learn and play by miraculously giving me so many pianos from age ten on. I set out to find a teacher and one we could afford. I also set out to learn more hymns, and before long, I knew a handful of them pretty well. The pianist at our church invited me to take turns playing piano with her; and for some reason, I jumped in, knowing I was not very skilled for the job. I was terrified but did it anyway. Desire outweighed my fear. Our music director was kind enough to ask me what I could play, and I would provide him with a list of hymns I was capable of playing. He would choose only from that list. Each week, as I kept practicing, my list of hymns grew longer, and I would give the director my updated list. After some time, I no longer gave him a list as I was able to play what he chose, especially with the few days' notice I was given.

During this time, I often felt I failed at my job, and I often wanted to run from the sanctuary crying, knowing I had not played an offertory or some song very well. Introductions were difficult for me, and

I frequently played them poorly. I often was embarrassed and humiliated, yet I kept playing. I had found a teacher I wanted to take lessons from, and she lived within walking or biking distance, which was helpful since I did not always have a car to use, but the monthly fee was difficult to afford. While I was struggling with all of this, trying to play better and thinking about lessons, a lady in our church approached me one Sunday about teaching piano to her daughter. I stood there in unbelief. I explained that I was still learning and trying to get lessons for myself. She simply said, "You know more than Michelle. Just teach her what you know." I asked her to let me think about it, and I went home totally dumbfounded that someone had asked *me* to *teach* piano. However, I mulled this over in my mind a few days, and it suddenly occurred to me that I could charge her the twenty-five dollars a month that I needed to take my own lessons, and we'd both be happy. I agreed to teach, set up a lesson time for her daughter and called, and set up lessons for myself.

I did start lessons and was enjoying every minute of them. I was learning and understanding some theory I had not understood before. I enjoyed my teacher who was just a little older than I was, and there she was, teaching with a young family all around her as I was doing in my home. She encouraged me to teach. I was enjoying practicing and putting in all the time I could find. You'll never believe what happened next. I discovered I was expecting child number three. Well, I did not stop lessons—mine or the ones I was teaching. I started with one student but had been getting calls to teach others, and I had a handful of students, obtaining a babysitter to help me with my young boys while I taught. I did have some morning sickness, but I was determined to keep on this time, and I continued. I played in a recital eight months pregnant. My pieces had been difficult to learn, but I managed. My little daughter came along, and my teacher moved. Lessons for me stopped for the time being. In the meantime, I was developing a studio of students and making an income to help with family finances. Teaching allowed me to be home with my young family, and I secured child-care help when needed. During this time, I was playing piano for worship services every week and developing more skills as a church musician. While teaching, I was learning more myself and eventually had more lessons.

There had been a short time when I looked for a job outside of our home, and in fact, I got one right away; but upon actually being offered the job, I panicked. Realizing how much I wanted to be home with my children, I did not take the job. I used an employment agency to help me find that job and met a very nice man who was my age and worked for the agency and who, upon learning I was teaching piano, told me about his mother who was also a piano teacher. When he learned I wanted more lessons, he gave me his mother's phone number. I didn't realize it then, but looking for an outside job and meeting this agent was very important because the lessons and relationship I ended up having with his mother is extremely significant in my life. She was a wonderful woman who took me under her wing.

My own mother had recently passed away, and she sort of mothered me. She had five grown children of her own, including her son who had steered me toward her. She taught me much about piano playing and threw me into many situations where I had to play and accompany. She always just believed I could do whatever she asked. I was forced to rise to the occasion over and over and had no choice but to see it through. The growth I achieved through her mentoring was huge—not just with playing piano, but with life in general. At one point, she taught not just me but all three of my children. She lived not in our city but a neighboring city, and we made the drive to her house once a week, all of us taking lessons on that day. My daughter grew to love her as much as I did. There was a time when our teacher suffered a stroke. All lessons stopped, but our friendship did not. It was during my study with this wonderful teacher that I first played for pay at a local boutique at Christmas time. I began to get more jobs like that—private parties and business dinners, weddings and wedding receptions, etc. That first gig at the boutique, I made seventy-five dollars after playing two hours. I was so excited that I called my teacher friend with excitement, and I remember asking her if I could now call myself a pianist. She said, "Yes, you certainly may!" I continued to call her after every piano-playing adventure to tell her and thank her. My playing career was growing, and my playing for church continued.

Our local city college offered music classes, and I enrolled in a musicianship class. Much to my surprise, I discovered it was a review for me. I had learned so much theory by then that I knew the material in the class. It was a good review, and I enjoyed the class, so I never felt it was a waste of time. One day, we had a substitute rather than our usual teacher. He mentioned he was a member of the Music Teachers Association of California (MTAC), and my ears perked up. I had heard of MTAC, and even visited a meeting once at the invitation of another teacher. I was not qualified to be a member, not having a four-year music degree, but I knew they offered a certification program that was basically the equivalent. To be in the study program, you had to be studying with a teacher who was a member of MTAC. After class, I asked the substitute about MTAC and lessons; and before long, I was enrolled in the program and studying under his guidance, attending lessons every week. I was allowed in MTAC as a provisional member and was very active as it was part of my schooling. The course was designed to last three to five years. I was stretching my study into the five years due to my family obligations, but as it turned out, due to a huge life upset, I had to quit the program before I had completed it. I had completed and passed all six written test areas but was still working on my performance exam when I was forced to quit. I resigned myself to the fact that I would not have the certificate but I would have all the knowledge I had gained, and that was what was important. Life went on without lessons or the program. However, one day a few years later, I was contacted by the state chairperson and was informed I could still finish the program if I desired. I had no idea I had that option. After some thought and knowing the time and expense involved, I decided to go for it and complete the program and gain my certification. Performance had been difficult for me. I suffered stage fright, and many of the pieces I studied were difficult to learn. I and my teacher, same one I had started the program with, followed all the guidelines, and I prepared my performance program. On the scheduled day, my husband and I traveled to the city where I was to take my performance exam, and I performed for the teacher appointed to evaluate me. I was uncomfortable with the person immediately as I stepped into her home. I was already nervous and didn't feel fully prepared. Feeling uncomfortable with her only made my nervousness worse. I played my program, was told I would be contacted by the state in a week or so, then went on my way. My gut told me I did not pass. My husband and I had planned a small vacation that weekend, and we continued on to our destination, to a friend's cabin in the mountains, but I felt upset. So many years and so much work and preparation and I felt I had failed. I was upset with myself that I would get so nervous, and I was sure it was all over, a waste of time. In fact though, when contacted, I was told I passed the majority, but I would need to relearn a classical piece and also a contemporary piece. Apparently, I had prepared far more than necessary and had spread myself too thin, plus we had misunderstood one requirement. So off I went with my teacher for further study to fulfill the last requirements. I did learn a new classical piece. It was Beethoven's "Funeral March." It was a Beethoven piece I had failed in the previous performance, and I wasn't eager to play his music again, but I loved the "Funeral March" and enjoyed it so much that I enjoyed practicing it. The contemporary piece was a suite of five short pieces. It was challenging but fun. I usually do my best performances with Romantic Era music, so I was outside my comfort zone on both.

Finally, it was time to be tested again. I was forty-three years old. Long career with the piano and still trying to get it right. As I was leaving my last lesson before the exam, my teacher offered to drive me to the city where I would perform. He was not aware that I was very uncomfortable driving there, but he said if it were him, he would rather be driven when facing a test than have to drive himself. I took him up on his offer, and a few days later, we headed out to drive the hour and a half to the home of the teacher who would hear me. It was not the same teacher as before. We both knew this teacher. I knew her because I had taken all my written tests in her home along with other testing students. I knew I would be comfortable with her.

It was a rainy day, and as we drove, a driver in front of us lost a ladder off the back of his truck bed, and it came flying straight at us. My teacher swerved to miss being hit, and the van we were in hydroplaned on the wet road. He kept control of his vehicle, and we continued on, adrenaline shooting through us at our near accident. It should have made me a nervous wreck, but somehow, I managed to control myself. I had to get through this performance and pass. We arrived in one piece and were greeted warmly. We did not speak of our near accident. I got settled in on the piano bench, my teacher went into another room, and the examining teacher sat nearby, then allowed me to begin. I played and finished and felt confident. Though students were not supposed to be given the results and told whether they passed or failed, this teacher said she wanted to tell me I passed with flying colors. The excitement both I and my teacher felt was high, and we were ready to celebrate. It had been ten years since I had first started the process to gain this certification, which I would now receive. I called my husband immediately, and he promised a celebratory dinner out that evening. I had already planned to take my teacher to lunch, so we headed home and out for lunch. He told me on the drive home that he couldn't believe how composed I stayed after our near accident. He confessed that he wasn't sure he could have performed after that. He said he was a nervous wreck after that near miss and was nervous for me. He wisely didn't let me know any of that beforehand.

I was flying high for weeks after passing that exam. You might remember a television commercial where a man so elated with lowering his cholesterol goes around telling anyone and everyone. I was like the cholesterol man. Anyone who said hello and even came close to asking how I was got told how I had passed my performance exam for my Cal Plan program and was receiving my certification as a piano instructor/performer with what was an equivalent to a four-year music degree. Never mind it took me ten years, mind you, with three years off in the middle. I had passed, and I was elated. I qualified as a full member of MTAC, which allowed both myself and my students many benefits.

After that time, I continued to teach thirteen more years, equaling almost thirty years total. I also took a year course in pedagogy at our local city college for even further teaching education. I continued to play for church worship services and ended up helping in several denominations. I played for funerals and weddings and receptions and dinner parties, at the local mall and other stores at Christmas time. I played keys in a five-piece band and, later, a six-piece band. I played duets for various events with a fellow piano teacher friend. I entered into a hymn-playing festival twice. I composed pieces. The instrument, the piano, that I first heard in church at nine years old and so caught my attention, had become a lifelong challenge, and a lifelong friend, taking me through many experiences and into many types of music. It was never easy but always rewarding and something I enjoyed. I am forever indebted to my teachers, starting with Laura Weiss, my very first piano teacher. I am especially indebted to Margaret Ruof who took me under her wing and always believed in me. I am also especially indebted to John Hord, who spent *endless* hours with me (much more than he got paid for) in the seven years (first four and then three) that he taught and mentored me in all areas of music and all the areas of the Cal Plan program of California. For his knowledge passed on to me and his patience and willingness to invest so much time in me, I am eternally grateful.

On this very day, as I am writing, my mothers' spinet piano sits against our living room wall, just inside the front door. Her picture sits upon it. I play it proudly and with many memories. I am thankful my parents bought it and gave me those first lessons and that my father saw fit to pass it on to me. Across the room sits an almost hundred-year-old, six-foot Chickering grand piano that we were able to purchase some years ago, secondhand from a church no longer using it. I never expected to own a grand piano, but again, a church came through with a piano just for me. Amazing.

Snow

It was winter, and Christmas was approaching. My husband and I decided to walk over to the festive little Christmas village that had been set up in the old town downtown area of our city. We lived in that area and had only to walk around the corner and down a block to join in the many festivities that our city presented. At this time, it was a Christmas display set up in a vacant parking lot that was used to hold many community events.

We entered through the gate and saw many Christmas trees, wreaths, various Christmas decorations displayed by vendors, and even a small ice rink. We lived in California where winters are warm and certainly no ice skating rink could exist outside. This "ice" was actually pieces of some special material that was put together like a jigsaw puzzle. We had never seen such a thing, but we had been hearing about it, and I watched one day as they were laying the fake ice. Apparently, it was smooth enough to skate on with regular ice skates, though a pro skater I knew said she would never use her good skates on anything but true ice. However, that night, there were a few skaters out there using their ice skates. It was a rather small area, but they were managing to actually skate. It was warm "ice" and a warm night. We barely needed long sleeves. We meandered through the Christmas village, heard Christmas music, and came upon some food vendors selling corndogs and sodas, popcorn and snow cones, and cotton candy. As we entered the little food court, it began to snow. It was warm snow on a warm night. I was startled and looked up to see two snow machines throwing out snow. It was fake snow, of course, and my reaction was to cry. Not sob, but tears stung my eyes, and I wanted to cry. I wanted it to snow. I wanted real snow.

For days and weeks, I had been longing for snow. Winter was coming, and I wanted cold days and snowy days like I remembered having as a child growing up in Kentucky. I wanted what I call a real winter, a season that is quite different than summer, spring, or fall. Where we lived, there was little difference between the seasons. I wanted cold days and biting cold nights and falling snow and to be able to wear coats and scarves and mittens and hats and boots. I wanted to wear all the things I knitted but found too warm to wear. I wanted to knit with wool and wear wool. I wanted to make snow angels and snowmen and eat snow cones made with real snow. I wanted to walk in the snow and throw snowballs. I wanted to see falling snow and see a snow covered ground. I simply wanted snow.

This desire for snow had been coming over me more and more intensely for quite some time. I had discovered a channel on our television that was currently playing what was called *Winter Wonderland*. It was a long video of all kinds of snow scenes played to music. There were scenes of heavy snowfall, snow-covered trees, frozen creeks, rabbits and other animals running through the snow, and penguins and polar bears on the ice and in icy waters. There were many cold and snowy scenes, both daytime and nighttime scenes. My husband was working some night hours at that time, and after he left, I would gather up my yarn and needles and sit on the couch with our dog and cat nearby and watch that channel, and tears would come. I would find the snowy scenery extremely beautiful, and something in me yearned for snow. There were times my husband and I would watch the winter scenes together. He noticed me crying and wondered what on earth was wrong with me. All I could say was, "I'm longing for snow. I want to live where it snows and snows a lot." He had also lived in a few snowy places as a child and had fond memories of snow.

We had been talking about moving on and off for quite some time, about eight years. At first, it was a passing thought and just chatter. As time went on, it began to feel like more of a possibility, but in the future. More time passed, and we began to speak of moving more frequently and even discussed places we might want to live. I especially started longing to move. I wanted to move somewhere very different than where we were. By the time I found that television channel, I was sure I wanted to live in snow, and my spirit and psyche cried out for it. I don't know exactly why, but they did. I knew I needed snow in my new home. I envisioned a house with a table where I would write while sitting next to a window where I would look out and see large trees in a snow-covered ground. I held that vision in my mind and started a search of where we might choose to live in. It occurred to me that we really did have a choice. We could move if we wanted and anywhere we wanted. And I started feeling that we should move. We needed a different environment.

As I started researching, my husband told me to choose the place and we would go there. He wanted to be kept abreast of where I was looking, of course, but we had agreed on the same top criteria. We also knew places we did not want to live. So I began to search in earnest and according to our list of criteria, which included four distinct seasons. I included a snowy winter as a must. That narrowed the search some already. There were areas we ruled out immediately; there were others I looked at—some where I had lived or visited as a child. I kept looking for our top five criteria: a much smaller population; slower pace of life; a higher elevation and different terrain, clean air (we lived in extremely dirty air and suffered because of it); and, last but not least, four distinct seasons, including snow in the winter. I looked and read about many states and many cities, but in each I researched, I ran across at least one of our five criteria not met. Of course, the United States is large, and there are many cities. I knew I could never read about all of them, but I kept searching. One day, in my search, I realized that neither of us, though we had both lived in or been in a number of states, had ever set foot in Montana, North Dakota, South Dakota, or Minnesota. Hmmm, I thought. What are those states like? One thing I did know, they had snowy winters.

I researched those northern Midwest states and varying cities in each, and one day, my searching found me lingering in North Dakota. I had once seen news about Fargo, North Dakota. It was the coldest city in the nation. I remembered looking at the scenes and marveling at the extreme low temperatures and the way of life in the winter. I looked up Fargo. It just about fit, but the population was still too large, plus it sat at a low elevation and the Red River flooded annually. Next I looked at Bismarck, the state capital. "This is it," I exclaimed to myself. North Dakota and probably Bismarck. All five top criteria were met, plus there was more about the area that was very appealing. After more reading and some discussion, we decided it would be Bismarck, North Dakota. There was one drawback. As we looked from afar for housing, we found there was none available. The recent oil boom wasn't all that far north, and housing had filled up. We talked to realtors and property management companies and could see finding a place to live would be extremely difficult. We had begun to mention to just a few family members of our intent to move to North Dakota and probably Bismarck, but now the city wasn't for certain. One day, as my husband sat at the computer looking around North Dakota, he hit upon the smaller town of Jamestown. I took a look at it and then studied the town further. Jamestown looked perfect, and the smaller population of just 15,000 sounded great. We were living in a city of over half a million in population. Fargo had 108,000; Bismarck, 60,000. Jamestown's 15,000 sounded much better. All criteria were met, and Jamestown got significant snow, even blizzards. We made our decision. Jamestown, North Dakota, it would be. We would be moving to North Dakota, having never set foot in the state, not knowing a soul, having no jobs and no home yet figured out. Still, we were going without fear or doubt, and we were excited. It felt very right and was going to be an exciting adventure. And the very next winter, we would experience snow for the first time since we were children. Now we needed to tell family and friends.

Telling family and friends proved to be a little difficult, and even emotional, on both sides. Our desire to move certainly wasn't a new idea to any of our family, and a few of our friends had heard us mention it at times. But now to state for certain that we were going to move and were moving far away and in the not-too-distant future was going to put a finality and reality to it, not just talk. We chose different times to tell our plans to different people. Some had plenty of time to digest the news; others, less time. I felt it would be most difficult for me to tell my father, our daughter, and our granddaughter.

My dad is a supportive father, and I felt he would understand our desire to go elsewhere, even if he didn't understand why. I felt he would consider it our freedom and choice. The difficulty for me was in knowing I was moving so far away from him. I didn't want him to feel I was deserting him or didn't care about him. It would be much more difficult to visit, and I would miss him. My daughter had always said she wanted to live right by me and never leave me. Now I was going to leave her. However, I had a deep sense that, if I never left, she would never search out her own life and go where she might want to. She would stay by me no matter what. When I expressed this sense to her through tears during one talk we had, she admitted I was right and she would probably not leave me. When I first told her about our move, she and I were on the train on the way to be with one of her brothers who was about to go through surgery. We had a lot of time to talk on the train ride. We agreed it was not the right time to tell her brother while he was facing the surgery and recuperation. He could be told later. We did tell both her brothers not long after, however. All three knew, and they were told when—in about eight months. My granddaughter, one son's daughter, was ten and taking piano lessons from me. I planned to tell her one day after her lesson. I waited for what seemed like a good day, and I prepared myself to tell her. I worried she would cry. Instead, I cried. Hard as I tried to tell her about it and make it sound exciting and a new place she could visit, and the snow in the winter, I cried. I cried quite a bit and told her it did not mean we didn't love her. I cried, but she took the news bravely, wiping her eyes to keep the tears away, and said, "It's okay, Grandma. I know you still love me." What's not to love about a child like that? What's not to love about a father, a daughter and sons, and a granddaughter who love you so much they can let you go because they want you to be happy, live where you choose, and follow your dreams, most significantly the dream to live where it snows and snows a lot? Family, friends, and students who might not have really understood why we wanted to move so badly or why we wanted such long cold winters, gave us their blessing anyway and accepted our decision. We started planning our move and put into motion the myriad of things that had to be done to accomplish such a move. It was huge. The reality of it became very clear to all. We had our last holiday season in California and talked of the snowy winter we'd enjoy the next year. We set about doing all the tasks that needed to be done and, week by week, moved closer to our departing date. It was going to happen.

On Saturday, June 9th, 2012, at six in the evening, we drove away from our home. The kids had been over a lot for a few days and had been there that day as the moving truck got loaded. They visited. They helped, and we all ate a fast-food meal together. It was a busy, tiring, and emotional day. I insisted that they all leave before it was time for us to pull away. I knew I would not easily handle waving good-bye to them and watching them as we drove off. I knew our daughter would not handle it well, and I wasn't certain about the boys. It was easier to say bye while we were still there and watch them drive off to their homes just as any other family visit. So at 6:00 p.m., we pulled away from our house with our dog, Melody, our one-year-old English bulldog, and headed out of California without looking back. We drove six hours and made our first overnight stop in Reno, Nevada. We saw nothing but our hotel bed and left fairly early in the morning. We made plenty of stops along the way both for ourselves and Melody, who turned out to be an excellent, fun, and easy traveler, but we were on a mission. We had Jamestown, North Dakota, and future snow, on our minds, and we wanted to get there.

We drove on through Nevada, Idaho, Montana, and then into North Dakota. We saw beautiful countryside and skies we'd never seen before. I'm not sure exactly what it was in me, but as we crossed the state line into North Dakota, the tears were back, stinging my eyes. We were arriving in North Dakota with a house, job, and friends yet to be found, yet somehow, I felt I had arrived home. Maybe it was just all the years of talking of moving, months of researching, and months of preparing to leave and finally arriving at our destination. Maybe it was the belief in the new lifestyle we were after. Maybe it was the promise of snow. We arrived on June 12. The day we arrived was a mild summer day, but there was the promise of a snowy winter.

We drove into Bismarck and stopped to get gas. We took a quick look at the city, but I absolutely knew it was not the right place even though, at first, we had chosen it. It was a pretty city, but it was busy and had busy roads. It felt terribly wrong in many ways. We both expressed the same feeling and said, "Let's go on to Jamestown as planned." We did. An hour and a half later, we arrived in Jamestown, descending a hill on the interstate that turned into a small road that went through Jamestown. As we drove down the hill, we saw tops of beautiful trees, striking church steeples, and a small, very inviting town. The hill was lined with pine trees, and the whole drive into the town was very picturesque. At the bottom of the hill, there in the center of town, we crossed a small pretty river called the James River. Before we even got all the way down the small hill, we said, "Yes! This is it! Jamestown, North Dakota." We were immediately smitten with our new town. We had driven three very long days and were ready to stop. We immediately looked for a motel to call home temporarily. In minutes, we found a motel we thought we'd try, named for the city, and paid for four nights. We had no idea how long we'd need to stay in the Jamestown Motel, but we arranged the four nights and were given a very simple but cozy room. It was sunny, warm, and windy, but winter would come and with it, snow. I held that thought constantly.

The very next day, we set off looking for a place to live. There was little to look at, and no one accepted pets. Per chance, the property management company we were talking to suddenly thought of a landlord who might have a house for rent. He did, and we went immediately to meet him and see it. It was perfect, having all we needed, and had even more that we'd dared to ask for in our prayers. The landlord even accepted our dog. We let Melody out of the car, and she greeted him using her very best behavior and manners, sitting very still and looking up into his eyes, just waiting for his response. She is an excellent dog but very exuberant when meeting new people. As we walked out to the car for this man who was maybe to become our landlord to meet Melody, I prayed a quick prayer that Mel would be calm and be found acceptable. I knew she could be excitable. Until that moment, we had never ever seen her sit so still upon meeting a new person. We have laughed about it many times. She's a smart dog, and I also think God must have given her a command to sit very still. Our new landlord accepted her immediately.

We were able to move into the house the very next day but knew we'd wait a month for our furniture and belongings. We made do with a few things we had brought along and with an air mattress the landlord loaned us. We loved our new home. We even had large trees around our house, which I could see from several windows. I looked out at them and tried to picture them in the deepest part of a snowy winter. That very same week, my husband found a job. I found work within a month, just as our furniture arrived and we were settling in. The very first week, we also found a church. We visited one near us and fell in love with the people. We never did visit another church. We didn't need to. With our new church home, we also immediately had new friends. Within twenty-four hours of arriving, we had found our home; within forty-eight hours, we were living in it; within a few days, at least one of us was working; and by the end of that same week, we had a church family. All of it was wondrously amazing. We settled in, started our jobs, and waited for winter while enjoying summer and fall.

Winter comes early in North Dakota. Autumn is short. We went through the summer marveling at many new things in our environment, such as daylight until almost 11 p.m. in midsummer, milder temperatures, thunderstorms, and a huge beautiful sky every day. We noticed the fresh and clean-smelling air, something we still can't stop talking about. Later, we had beautiful color changes with the arrival of fall and a major dip in temperatures. We enjoyed more rain and a lot of wind. Wind is very common in North Dakota. As the temperatures dropped to single digits and subzero temperatures, we were watching for snow. I had an everyday expectation that snow might fall, and I warned my boss if the first snow fall was during work hours, I would have to leave momentarily to go outside and experience it. He and my coworkers thought I was crazy, but they also accepted my excitement. As it turned out, our first snow fall was on a Saturday before Halloween. We had pumpkins on our front porch steps. They froze and were covered with snow. I was ecstatic. That first snow fall wasn't much, but it gave a light covering, and I found it glorious. I found it exciting and energizing to see it snow and to feel the cold air. We were experiencing colder temperatures than we ever had before. All my knitted goods came out, and I wore a wool scarf and hat. We bought boots and all the needed extra layers for cold temperatures. We had emergency kits in our cars, as instructed by helpful new friends and neighbors. It wasn't unheard of to get stuck in a snowstorm and possibly become stranded. Sleeping bags, blankets, extra clothing, water, food, a candle in a can, and matches were all a must. Flashlight and flares too. We prepared our cars. New to us too were needing window scrapers for our cars and snow shovels to clear our walkways and driveway. Neighbors with snow blowers helped us out as well.

There were many practical things to do to be prepared for the snow, and we did all those and didn't mind, but what we so enjoyed was the beauty of the falling snow piling higher and higher and the freshly covered yards and fields blanketed in white. The trees were magnificent, sometimes holding inches of snow on their bare limbs, or on certain days, when conditions were just right, they looked like crystal trees—sparkling. My favorite days were the crystal-tree days, the trees looking like standing icicles but with a sleeping tree underneath the ice covering. When I was a child, I was disappointed when my family visited the Petrified Forest, and all I saw were pieces and chunks of fossilized trees. In my mind's eye, I had falsely pictured a standing forest of petrified trees. I was sorely disappointed. It's a bit of family history we sometimes chuckle over—my misconception and disappointment. But crystal-looking trees standing tall, sparkling in the North Dakota winter on those special days when conditions are just right, have satisfied my longing to see a forest of petrified trees. On those cold, icy days, everywhere you look in the town, you see frozen, as if petrified, sparkling trees. They are just beautiful. It's a winter wonderland.

That first snow came on October 27. It didn't stick around long, but by mid-November, we had snowfalls and temperatures that left snow on the ground, and it piled up. We had snow on the ground till the end of April. Our last but biggest snowstorm arrived on April 14, when much of the state had a blizzard. We were in slightly milder blizzard conditions. That first winter, I was excited every time the snow fell. I found it exhilarating as I did the very cold subzero temperatures. The chill factor took us as low as negative forty, though that was by no means the lowest it might go. North Dakota is cold. We enjoyed every minute of our first winter. We were warm and comfortable inside. We watched as ferocious storms came through, blowing heavy snowfalls sideways. We watched on calm and still days as large snowflakes silently fell, covering all, and the world was hushed and quiet and white. Those days are a thing of wonder. The sight can leave you speechless.

I made snow angels in one of the earliest snows. We made snowballs when the snow was wet enough, and one day, I made a tiny snowman. I made snow cones out of real snow. Our dog had never seen snow, and we enjoyed watching her maneuver in it and play and eat it. She had very limited time outside as it was too cold for man or beast much of the winter, but she did experience and learn about snow. We learned to drive in snow, and each experienced a few "exciting" moments with that. Fortunately, we live only one mile from both of our workplaces and just travel a small neighborhood street straight to work. I wanted to get "snowed in," but that didn't happen, at least not to us. It did for some in more country areas and is a common occurrence.

As I write this, it is October again. We went back to California in June for our daughter's wedding. We saw family and friends and spent Father's Day with my dad. One son traveled back with us for a ten-day visit. So far, we have been back just that one time and were driving back the same week we had been driving to North Dakota the year before. Our daughter and her husband and son now live in Virginia. They moved, our daughter taking a job she wanted. Would she have been willing to go after that job and move if we were still in California? We'll never know.

This will be our second winter in North Dakota. It just so happens that snow flurries are expected tomorrow, a Sunday. Temperatures have dropped to the thirties and below. Each day, I watch and wait, looking for that first snow. Most old timers here wish it would hold off a while, a long while, but it cannot come too soon for me. Maybe after a few years, I too will tire of the snow, but as I tell everyone, let me enjoy it for now. I'm looking forward to those quiet, hushed days when those large snowflakes fall silently and peacefully, covering our world white, snow piling higher and higher. I'm looking forward to snow play and snowy walks. I'm looking forward to snowstorms, even a blizzard, and I even look forward to shoveling snow or getting "snowed in." One thing we don't do is travel in the heavy snows. We take every precaution to not get stuck in a storm, and at least to be as prepared as possible. Those emergency kits are going in our cars.

I am eagerly watching for those first flakes. It will be the beginning of a long winter. Six months of winter is common here. This year, our dog will know about snow, but we have a new kitten, and it will be a first-time experience for her. When the very first snow falls, we will take her outside to watch her reaction and to let her chase snowflakes. As last year, I will be camera ready for all snowfalls. Again, I will try to capture a shot of the spectacular, sparkling crystal trees as they stand in their silent frozen glory. We will have a snowy winter again, no one knows how mild or how severe, but we will have snow. I will enjoy it, respect it, and take note of its beauty.

PS
Sunday arrived and so did the first snowfall!

Mom

On any given morning, I would awake and hear my mother in the kitchen. This was especially true during weekdays and most especially during school days. Weekends and summer days could vary slightly. I would get up and get dressed then enter the kitchen to find breakfast ready—cold cereal, oatmeal, or eggs, and toast, maybe pancakes, waffles, or muffins. Juice and milk were always available. The table was set with all my dad, brother, sisters, and I needed. We always got breakfast before school, and while we were dressing and eating, Mom was already well into making our lunches. Brown paper bags or, sometimes, lunch boxes lined the kitchen counter, and Mom would be making sandwiches and filling our sacks and boxes with them. Added to our lunches were chips or crackers, fruit, and homemade cookies—almost always, homemade cookies. Sometimes we had a thermos packed along with our lunch, but usually, we bought milk at school. It was as cheap as a nickel back then. I think it actually cost less than a nickel, but I cannot remember the exact price for a carton of milk during those school days in the 1960s. Once in a while, we bought lunch, but that was not the norm. I had few worries in those days and didn't think a lot about the things Mom did. It was just the way it was. Looking back now, I know how fortunate I was to have a mother and to have one who was a stay-at-home mom and to have one who was so devoted to my father and to my brother, sisters, and me.

Our clothes were clean and ready for wear, usually laid out the night before. Our breakfast was provided, we were helped with our hair and getting coats on and our things together, and off we went to school on a school bus. The bus stop was down the street and around the corner—not far. Our family had one car, and my father usually took it to his school and work. He was a student at the time and was also working. On days my mother needed a car, she and my father would work it out, or he would pick her up. Most often, my mother was home and did not have a car.

My mom came from a generation of stay-at-home moms, and most of my friends had mothers at home, it seemed. I was a stay-at-home mom too while my kids were growing up, but times were already changing, and there was always that subtle push to go out and get a job. As I reflect back on my growing-up years, I feel very fortunate and grateful to have grown up at a time and place when being a mom at home was not only possible but valued. The chores and many things my mother did while we were growing up are invaluable. I know now that all she did to keep our household fed, running, and nurtured was no small task.

My mom did all the normal things of that day and era. She did laundry and often hung it out to dry, prepared three meals a day, baked most every day, sewed many of our clothes, mended, and took us shopping along with my dad for other clothing. She cleaned the house, did minor repairs, painted, helped take care of the yards, grew flowers, tended to pets, paid bills, wrote letters, dealt with phone calls and knocks on the door, befriended neighbors, talked to our teachers, and, along with my father, attended open houses and parent-teacher conferences. She saw that we got our homework done and made sure we had time to do it. She made sure we had all the resources we needed to do our everyday homework and special projects. She made cupcakes and brought them to school for our class birthday celebrations. At home, she made us the birthday dinner of our choice and the birthday cake of our choice, decorated by her. She made sure we had valentine cards to pass out to classmates, goodies and gifts for school Christmas parties, and etc. The list is endless. Most important to me is the fact that my mom was there. She was present in every facet of my life—morning, noon, and night. Long before I was up, she was up; and long after I was in bed, she wasn't.

When I was sick and needed to stay home, my mom was there. She didn't have to make arrangements to be home. She was already going to be home. There may have been some times when one of us being home sick interrupted her plans for the day, but nevertheless, mom was home. I remember being allowed to lay and sleep on the family room couch when sick. The TV was in that room, and being home laying around, I was allowed to watch some TV. Sometimes, my mom had a show she wanted to watch, and we would watch it together. That was a perk to being home. When I was sick, Mom would oversee my condition and watch my temperature and fever. She would feed me soup, Jello, and whatever might make me feel better and provide some nourishment. I was given many cold drinks and cool cloths at times. I was allowed to sleep as much as needed. I had no worries. Mom would call the school and explain I was sick. Mom was there to take care of me, and all I needed was right there. I had nothing to worry about or do except rest and get better. Not all children had or have that worry-free care I now know.

I was given certain chores as a child—simple things, such as cleaning the cat litter box, setting the table, drying dishes and putting them away, folding clothes, polishing shoes, picking up toys, etc. Nothing too harsh or extraordinary, just things that helped. My mom and dad taught me how to do many tasks.

I have one particular memory that is painful but special in its own way and forever locked in my brain. We had a litter of kittens and had been confining them to the back screened in porch. Mom would put a card table up at the door leading to the kitchen so that she wouldn't have to close the door, but the kittens were still prevented from running wild into the house. They were tiny but active. One morning, my mom asked me to put the table up for her. I did as asked, but being fairly young and not very experienced, I did not pull the legs out on the table when I put it up. I just propped it against the doorway like I thought my mother did. I didn't realize it wasn't a safe situation, and my mom was unaware of my lack of understanding or how the table had gone up. It wasn't long before we heard a crash. A kitten, or kittens, had knocked the table over, and one kitten had been smashed and killed when the table hit its tiny head. It was not my first time to experience the death of an animal, but it was certainly my first time to be the cause of a death. I was horrified, heartbroken, and sobbing. Seeing the situation, Mom realized I had not put the legs out and that was why the table had fallen. I sobbed and sobbed because I had killed the little kitten. My vivid memory is of me sitting on the stairs leading to our upstairs rooms and crying my heart out while my mom held me and let me cry, telling me all the while that it was not my fault, just an accident. I remember her taking full blame for the incident, saying she should have shown me how to put the table up so it wouldn't fall. Over and over, she said it wasn't my fault as she comforted me as we sat together on the stairs. It was a very sad day for me and a bitter pill to swallow knowing it was my action, or lack of, that killed that kitten. The kitten was innocent. That's how I saw it. My mother saw me as innocent. That's all I remember of that day, the most important being that my mom did not blame me or become angry but was there to comfort me and did. That interaction is forever locked in my memory.

During my fourth-grade year, which was a good year for me after a difficult third grade, we had a poster contest. I'm not certain if it was just my class or several classes who participated in the contest, but I think it was all the fourth-grade classes. I set out to make a poster. It was an assignment we all had to do. I was eager to make my poster, but I also had no idea what to do, and that kind of thing was not my strong suit. My mother, on the other hand, was an excellent artist, including poster making. I don't remember what the poster was about or what we did, but my mother helped me with that assignment, seeing I was stuck. I have a suspicion now that she enjoyed helping me with it because she enjoyed that type of art. I took my poster. It was hung with all the others. Judging day came, and the winners were announced. I won the first-place award. The blue ribbon. Of all the posters, I won first place. I don't remember what other award there was, if any, except for the blue ribbon and recognition; but when I should have been happy, I was not. In fact, I was upset. My mom greeted me upon my arrival home and immediately noticed something was wrong. She asked me what was wrong, and through tears, I told her I had won the poster contest. She asked why I was upset about it, and I had to tell her I didn't feel I deserved the award because I really didn't make it, at least not alone. She had helped me with the idea and the doing of it, and I didn't feel I had earned the award. Seeing my discomfort and tears, Mom hugged me and apologized for helping me. She was very sorry for helping me as much as she did. I remember standing there in our living room, where Mom had come to greet me, hugging each other, me feeling underserving of my award, and Mom feeling sorry she had helped me and robbed me of doing my own work and feeling proud of my award. What I remember is our hugging, Mom understanding my feelings, and her apology to me. I don't know that she needed to apologize, but she did.

Sometimes, I was in trouble with my mom. More than once. A friend was over one afternoon, and we got into a big fight. I was very annoyed with this friend. I lost my patience with her, and next thing I knew, we were rolling on the floor, hitting each other. We were having this fight when my mom came and broke it up. She sent my friend home and sent me to my room with stern words. She was rightfully upset at our behavior and put a stop to it. I do not remember what the fight was about, only that I was exasperated with my friend and decided to let her have it. This friend is still a friend today, forty-five years later. She does not remember the fight at all. Thankfully, she was forgiving. My mom did not put up with behavior such as that fight and taught me it was no way to treat a friend.

Mom also had no patience for me throwing rocks and hitting my sister in the eye. I did not mean to hit my sister and didn't know I was throwing the rock right at her. Most likely, my aim was poor. I felt I was treated very unfairly when my sister ran crying to Mom, and I got sent to my room to think about what I had done and the harm I might have caused. I was upset because I did not intentionally hurt my sister, but I was also upset, at least a little bit, that I had hurt her. I sat in my room. Actually, I sat in the back of my walk-in closet feeling sorry for myself. My mom didn't leave me there too long. She took care of my sister's injury then came to talk to me. She was calm and explained to me why she had gotten upset and sent me to my room. She explained why throwing rocks was not the best thing to do, but she acknowledged that I did not intend to cause harm. Mom smoothed things over, and I felt better. These type of events I have mentioned take time and effort from a mother. My mom was there and took the time and effort to deal with each situation and to teach us something.

My parents were great at letting me have friends over. My mom and dad would go out of their way to make my friends happy and comfortable in our home. Many times, I was allowed to have a friend spend the night or allowed to go to a friend's house for the night. I attended many slumber parties and also hosted many slumber parties. My parents let me have four or five girls over, and Mom prepared delicious foods and snacks with my dad's help and participation. They prepared scavenger and treasure hunts, and everyone had fun and was made to feel welcome. We stayed up all hours of the night, of course. I remember one particular slumber party when we stayed up all night on a Friday night then, bright and early Saturday morning, decided to jog around the block. Apparently, we could be heard all over the neighborhood, and my mom was not too happy to hear us making such racket so early on a Saturday morning. We were sent inside soon as she could get a hold of us, and we were made to quiet down.

Whereas the earlier kitten story still makes me cry, this story makes me laugh. As a mother myself, I know how trying slumber parties can be. Mom was a trooper to allow all of us girls together in her house. We absolutely did have fun then spent the next day exhausted. That is the way of slumber parties.

When I was in eighth grade and going to graduate from my school, I needed a graduation dress. My mom made me a dress. As I mentioned earlier, she sewed quite a bit, and it was less expensive in those days to make a dress than buy one. I was happy with home-sewn dresses, and I remember well the lavender-colored dress Mom made for me. I believe I may have gotten new shoes to go with the dress. Both the dress and shoes could be worn again for Sunday wear, or even to school. It was not feasible to have a dress that could be worn only once. I liked the dress and wore it many times. A picture of me in that dress hangs in my house today; it is within a collage of pictures Mom once put together for me.

When my high school graduation came around, I needed a dress again. Mom took me shopping at Sears that time, and we found a dress, for the right price, that I really liked. I knew Mom was relieved when we found a nice one, which I liked, that fit into the family budget. Again, it could be worn many times for various occasions. I wore that dress for my graduation, wore it afterward, and was still wearing it after I was married and had my first son four years later. I wore it even longer. I wore it till it wore out. I remember my mom once saying that she wished she could easily go buy a pair of new socks for herself without having to worry about the family budget. We were far from poor, but money was tight and carefully spent. Dad worked, but Mom was a full-time homemaker. One income had to suffice, and it wasn't always easy, especially for Mom, who gave up much of what she needed or might have liked to have in order for the rest of us to have what we needed. I know she did. I know she did it happily, but I know, at times, it was hard on her as well.

One very fun and "naughty" memory I have with my mother is a grocery-shopping trip we made together one afternoon. Groceries were budgeted in, and there was only so much per week for food. Mom bought carefully and wisely and made it stretch. She cooked from scratch, baked from scratch, and made foods that went a long way. On this particular day, after loading the grocery sacks into the car, Mom said, "Why don't you bring that Honeycomb cereal up front, and we'll eat a few as a snack on the way home." I was more than happy to do that and sat the cereal box between us. In went Mom's hand and in went my hand over and over. The drive home was not very far, but as we arrived, Mom realized we had eaten the entire contents of the box. She said we had been very naughty but it would be our secret. I laughed and was all for having a secret. We giggled at being so naughty as to finish off a box of family cereal that was supposed to last for the week. We never mentioned it to anyone, at least I didn't. It was our secret. Mom may have told Dad, I don't know, but that is one of my favorite memories with Mom.

As a teenager, there were many times mine and Mom's relationship was strained. I suppose it was normal, but some of it makes me feel sad. I know now I could have been more helpful and kind, more understanding and definitely more appreciative. Mom did not always share her feelings easily, and neither did I. That led to misunderstandings more than once. As I got older, I wanted to do things more my own way as well, and that led to conflict at times. I suppose all of that is normal, but I'm not sure it being normal makes it any better or right. Above all, no matter what, I know Mom loved me and I did her.

When I got engaged and my wedding was being planned, many changes started taking place. These were difficult for Mom and me. There was pain amongst the joy. Even so, my mom and dad threw us an engagement party. I think back on that and realize how giving that was. Mom did a lot to make that party nice for me. When it came time for bridal showers, my mom was right there with me. I think those were a bit difficult for both of us. As my wedding was planned, my mother took the brunt of the work. Mom made my wedding dress and veil, all four bridesmaid dresses, and worked out flowers with friends and their gardens as well her own flower garden. Mom made my cake and made sure all the necessary things were done. I was young. When I look back at that, I know what she did was astronomical. She and I were struggling with our feelings, and yet she was deep into making my wedding nice and beautiful for me. I don't believe I ever thanked her enough. I know I didn't.

As years passed, my mom was involved with my children as much as she could be from afar. She and Dad sent gifts and cards and money. They sent gifts and cards and money to me too. They made visits, and we visited them. Even after my mother was very sick, fighting cancer, she came and watched all three children when my husband and I needed to be away a few days. That was an extreme act of love as I realized later. My mom was much too ill for that job just then, but I thought she was well enough to do it since she came. We had a stressful encounter that hurt us both deeply, but I was not understanding just how ill and tired she was, and she was not understanding an issue in my life. How could she? I didn't tell her.

My mom became sick with breast cancer, diagnosed at age fifty-five. She put up a strong fight for five years. I imagine she did it mostly for my dad and us four kids. She suffered greatly but with grace. It is difficult to watch someone you love struggle and suffer as she did. We were all with her at the time of her passing. We all had a chance to sit with her and talk with her. One night, as I sat with her and spent some time with her, she labored to tell me something. We had already talked some, and I knew we were in a good place, both having already forgiven the other for misunderstandings. We didn't figure them all out, but we did forgive. That night, as she labored to tell me something, I listened closely but, at first, couldn't make it out. Then I heard it. Mom said, "I love you." I said, "I love you." I'm so glad I understood my mom say those last words to me, yet when I look back at the events I have written here and remember more that are not written here, I already knew Mom loved me. She spent her life showing me. No matter what difficulties we might have had understanding each other, love is in the doing. Love is action.

If I could have my mom back for just one day, I would make her a nice lunch or maybe take her out for lunch. I'd tell her many things, listen to whatever she wanted to share, then I'd take her shopping for socks.

Monkeys in the House

There are monkeys in our house. Monkeys everywhere. We live with two monkeys, and at times, it seems the monkeys have taken over. We got our first monkey when she was only twelve weeks old. The very first thing she did was leave a mess on our couch. I thought, "Oh boy, here we go, house breaking." She was just a baby and had to learn about such things. That first monkey grew and learned with our patience and training. She is a very smart monkey. By the time she was two, we decided to get a second monkey. Also a female. She was only eight weeks old when we got her but is now six months at this writing. Play, play, play. This second monkey likes to play, and the monkeys like to play together. They can create quite a stir in the house with their play. They run and chase each other, grab at each other, bite playfully at each other, wrestle, and chase toys together. They also sleep together so sweetly. Our monkeys are inside most of the time, but sometimes, they cry to go outside, and then we take them in the yard to play or go walking. Our monkeys are fun and funny and keep us very entertained. They are silly monkeys but are loving creatures, devoted to each other and to us. We love our monkeys.

Our oldest monkey's name is Melody. She is not only smart but quite a good monkey. She is very obedient. This monkey, Monkey Melody, is our English bulldog. Mel, or Monkey Head as we often call her, was given to us. Certain characteristics of her face, like her flat nose and big lips, remind us of a monkey. I also call her Marshmallow Head because when she lays with her head on her paws, her head and lips look soft and smooshy like a melting marshmallow. I have a marshmallow in my hot cocoa every morning and always give Mel a small bite of marshmallow. I say it's so she won't lose her marshmallow head. She is quite aware of when the marshmallow bag is opened and watches intently, waiting to see if she'll get her bite. She's such a funny monkey and aware of everything around her.

As I said, Melody was a gift. My husband had always wanted an English bulldog, but they are an expensive breed. Buying one was quite a bit beyond the budget. Friends of ours who had bulldogs and were involved in breeding ended up with the last puppy of a litter from a breeder they knew. Selling all the puppies had proven difficult, and the last puppy was given away. Our friends, in turn, decided to give her to us if we wanted her. We did. We gave her a name and fell in love with her. She proved to be funny and entertaining right away, and oh so smart. We had been told the breed was smart and also read that English bulldogs bond more with people than other dogs and are, in many ways, more like people. It is very true.

Melody showed us right away how smart she is, even with her puppy needs and lessons to learn. She was and is a very easygoing dog. We did not have a choice in the day she was delivered to us, and that very night, we had to be away about nine hours. We set her up in our small bathroom and gave her bedding and water and a toy and newspaper on which she could take care of her business. We gated her in and kissed her good-bye, wondering what might happen and if she would cry or bark. When we arrived home all those hours later, little Monkey Melody was quietly sitting on her bed, everything was in order, and the paper had been used a few times. She eagerly greeted us, and we praised her and loved her. With no other room available for her and for training, the bathroom became her room, and never once did she cry at night when we put her in it at bedtime. Only in the morning after we were up and if we took too long getting to her did she begin to cry to be let out. We figured that her time living alone in a kennel, after the other puppies were gone, helped her be used to the solitude and small room. Mel is a purebred English bulldog, but her markings were not considered top-notch. We consider her top-notch.

Melody shared our life with two senior dogs and a couple aloof cats that first year. She was ignored by the old dogs and tried to play with the cats but spent most of her time with us. As we had read, she considered us her pack. She considered us leaders of the pack too, as was evident in certain episodes and in training her. She understood we were in charge.

One day, when Mel had left another "pile" for me at the backdoor, I took her to that door and said, "Melody, the next time you need out, you cannot just stand here and hope we notice." Though we did watch her like a hawk in those early days, I continued and said, "When you want out, you come to this door and say woof." I looked her straight in the eye and said again, "To go potty (which we call it) you have to come here and say woof." Then I cleaned up her "uh-oh," which is what we said when anything naughty happened. Not too much later, I was busy in the kitchen when I heard "woof." I looked around the corner to the backdoor and saw Mel standing there, looking like she wanted out. I went straight to her and opened the door. Out she went and did her business in the yard. Melody got a lot of praise for that. I only needed to tell her one time, and she got it. That amazed me. She has done it every time ever since. Smart monkey. I have told her other things that I am positive she understood as well.

Monkey Melody is a sensitive monkey. She has feelings and shows them, and sometimes, she is quite funny about it. One afternoon, when she was still young, I caught her chewing our garden hose. That was a big "uh-oh." I scolded her and took it away and sent her inside. I scolded her very sternly, and she understood she had done something very bad. I went inside to find Monkey Mel in her room, sitting in the corner on her bed with her head hanging low as if she felt shame and sadness. I told her she had done a big uh-oh. She wouldn't look at me. I left her. As my husband and I were fixing our dinner, we looked in at Mel through the crack in the door. She was still sitting there in the corner with her head down, looking very contrite. We quietly laughed. After a few more minutes, I went in and talked softly to her, petted her head, hugged her neck, and told her she was forgiven and that she could come out. She just sat there, head down. I told her all was well and that she could come out. She didn't budge. We went on and ate our dinner. There was no move from Mel. I went back in to see her and hugged her neck and told her it was okay, that she was a good girl and could come out. She barely looked at me. I left her again. My husband told her she could come out, all was okay. She didn't budge. A little bit later, we heard her stirring. Slowly, she came out of her room and sheepishly walked into the room where we were. We assured her she was welcomed, but she gave herself a place on the floor rather than on the blanket up on the couch with us. She acted unworthy of the treat of being on the couch. Slowly, throughout the evening, she forgave herself and us and, eventually, was on the couch, snuggled up next to me. All was right in her world again. I learned she did not need that stern of a scolding to understand the wrong done. Time after time, she would put herself in the corner, either on her bed or in an "out of the way" corner in our living room if some uh-oh occurred. She would do this whether she was the cause or not. She would go to the corner when afraid also. If we found her in the corner, we would ask her what happened and start looking for damages or trouble. Sometimes, we found something out of place or the cats had knocked something over. Monkey Mel does not like things out of place or new things to appear. When either happens, she will either bark, hide in the corner, or both.

When Melody was two, we decided it was time for a second monkey. Our two older beloved dogs and one old cat had already passed on, and the last cat we had was given to friends when we made a major move. We had missed having a cat, and we knew Melody would enjoy having one. She always seems to enjoy felines. One happy day, we brought home a tiny kitten—our second monkey. We had no idea how much of a monkey she would be. Kittens are playful and silly, and Monkey Merri was every bit of that and more, yet not destructive. Our biggest curiosity was how she and Melody would get along. Melody is a very heavy dog, and Merri was a tiny kitten. She was barely two pounds up against a solid forty-five pounds. Mel could hurt Merri badly if she wanted to. She didn't. The kitten was wary of Mel but not afraid. She was courageous enough to keep Mel at a distance if Mel dared get too close, making her uncomfortable. They were constantly together and quickly grew to know and trust each other. Within one week, little Monkey Merri was snuggled up next to Monkey Melody in the dog bed. It was now the monkey bed. They were pals, and the fun began.

Our dog and kitten have become best buddies. They remind me of my favorite childhood cartoon, Chopper and Yakky. Chopper was a big English bulldog, and

Yakky was a little duck who Chopper called his little buddy. I loved watching that cartoon, and now, I have my own version of Chopper and Yakky. If Melody had been a male dog, we would have named her Chopper. Maybe in turn, we would have named Merri, Yakky. In any case, we have our own version of the cartoon characters.

Melody and Merri run around our house, chasing each other. Merri is not at all afraid to sneak up on Mel, jump on her, and start the play. Mel is game to play and goes after her. As my parents used to say and as I said to my children when play got too rough, "Somebody is going to end up crying." It was often true, and it is sometimes true that kitty will let out a yelp and run and hide, or Mel might let out a yelp and jerk away. Neither has ever hurt the other on purpose or caused more than a moment's poke or scratch or just a yell of "time out." Monkey Merri knows how to get Monkey Mel riled up, and Mel knows how to get the kitty running for cover. They will play till kitty is wet with dog slobber and Mel is winded. It's good exercise and play for them. It makes them happy. The next thing you know, they are snuggled up together, taking a nap and resting up. Often, we will see Merri licking Mel's head and ears or snuggling up as if Mel is her mama cat. Mel appears to enjoy the licking and often will, very gently, nuzzle her back in return.

When Melody is taken out for a walk or goes in the car with one of us, Merri cries to get out and go too. Since she is still a baby and since our city has an ordinance against letting cats roam (if you can believe that),

Merri only goes out on a leash and under supervision. She gets a turn outside once or twice every day and chases every bug or leaf or blade of grass that moves. She climbs trees as far as the leash will go and does all the things cats like to do. Inside, we play games with each of them. My husband has a slipper game he plays with Mel, slapping his slippers together and getting her excited and ferocious sounding. Merri chases after toys we dangle for her and jumps high over and over. Merri steers clear of Mel's slipper game. The racket made is a bit overwhelming for her, I think, but Mel tries to join in Merri's jumping games, all forty-five rock-solid pounds of her. Merri was already litter-box trained when we brought her home and has never made a mess where she shouldn't. She is quite tidy and is very possessive when I clean her litter box. She considers it her personal property and watches my every move, supervising and checking things out until I have it all back in place. Merri thinks all rooms, all furniture, and all objects exist for her pleasure, though she truly has been a good monkey and has not damaged anything. We did kitten-proof our home to some extent, however, and some doors stay closed.

Monkey Merri is growing and looks like a cat now. She doesn't look like a monkey as Mel does, but she sure acts like one, jumping here, there, and everywhere, leaping into the air as she does, and chasing toys or imaginary things. Mel was originally afraid of the stairs and had no experience in going up or down a flight of stairs. We spent some days teaching her and helping her until she no longer cried and whined but would run right up and run right down. Merri, on the other hand, had no trouble with stairs, of course. Pitter patter, pitter patter right up or down she goes, as agile as any cat, or monkey.

Some of my favorite moments in the day are in the very early morning, right after my husband gets up and lets Merri upstairs into our room. During the night, she sleeps downstairs with Melody. I lay waiting, and in a moment, I hear the familiar pitter patter of Merri's little feet running up the stairs to greet me and sleep with me. I get another two hours of sleep. She snuggles up to me cheek to cheek and lays her paws gently on my face, purring all the while. I love feeling her soft fur and hearing her contented purr. Both make me feel comforted and happy. Soon, her purring slows then stops, and I know she is sound asleep. I go back to sleep feeling her soft little body snuggling mine. It feels nice and so special that she should treat me so lovingly. When 5:00 a.m. arrives, Merri starts to stir, somehow knowing it's time to get up, and she wakes me with her play. Once she and Mel are both fed and Mel has gone outside and back in, my shower is done, and I have my hot cocoa in hand, the three of us head back upstairs. I steady my cup and hold on to the rail while Merri runs up, making her pitter patter sounds, and Mel thuds loudly up the stairs, moving her heavy body rather well and with no fear. I have already prepared the bed with her blanket so she can lie on the bed with kitty and me. The three of us huddle together, and I kiss their heads and necks. I love snuggling these special creatures entrusted to me for their care, and I love how they love me back, grateful and happy. It amazes me how three different creatures—human, canine, and feline—can live under one roof in such harmony and trust. They are truly a precious gift from God. They bring joy, safety, and better health with their love and devotion and with the acceptance of all we are. Their loyalty, tolerance, and forgiveness toward us know no bounds. I kiss their faces and tell them they are good, then I drink my cocoa while they begin their morning play. They first play on the bed then all over the upstairs, making all kinds of racket. They carry on until one cries stop or one needs to rest. Then they rest a while, side by side, with total trust in each other. So begins the day with monkeys in the house.

The Almighty Dollar

When I was a child, holidays seemed very special. They were times set aside to stop the normal week and flow of things to celebrate and remember special people or events. Having these special days not only allowed time for reflection but allowed us a break in our schedules. It was refreshing as well as special. Sunday was a day that was always special. For my family, it was a different day than all the rest. It was a day that stores and many businesses closed and a day to go to church and worship then rest at home in the afternoon. It was a day set aside each week to break the usual routine and give us a rest before we started a new week. There were things about Sunday that could be tiring. We still got up and out the door early. My mom cooked a big, special pot roast meal, and she and my dad had responsibilities at church, but it was still a day different from the rest. We needed that break, and we needed the day of worship set aside from the normal week. Weekly and throughout the year, we all still need these breaks in routine, yet they seem to have mostly disappeared.

When I was a child, holidays that changed our routine were not only the big ones, such as Easter, Thanksgiving, Christmas, and New Year's Day. The Fourth of July was observed as was Labor Day, Veteran's day, Memorial Day, Lincoln's birthday, and Washington's Birthday. These were days that not only banks and the post office observed, but schools were closed and stores were closed, as were many restaurants. People found value in observing these days, taking a break from the norm and being still and quiet or partaking in some special recreation. There was time to think about what each holiday was about. It was much like taking a moment of silence to give precedence and thought to something very important—something important enough to stop us from our normal tasks. Somewhere along the way, our society decided these days were no longer very important. As years passed, society, retailers especially, decided these were opportune days to make another buck, or thousands of bucks. The almighty dollar became more important than any person or event we were previously giving our time and thought to. Sunday was included, and as retailers sought more money, stores no longer closed on Sunday either.

As this shift took place, a number of things happened. Our society no longer gave reverence to things that previously received our attention. Not only were people enticed to shop on Sundays and holidays by the enormity of sales being advertised, but all those who worked in retail became prisoners to the new schedule of every day being a workday. No longer could one count on weekends or at least Sunday off. No longer could one expect to be free and home for a Thanksgiving or Christmas gathering with family. Various family members working in retail did not share the same schedule and certainly did not have the freedom of those not working in retail. As one who is currently working in retail, after a thirty-year career of self-employment and setting my own schedule as I saw fit, I struggle even more so now with this love of the almighty dollar. Every major holiday and every special day, Sunday included, I struggle with this compulsion that retailers have to open their doors on what I consider the sacred days. My philosophy of life and my belief system do not match with retail. Though I like my job in other ways and enjoy many of my coworkers and customers, I encounter constant personal conflict. For now, as I work this job, I am somewhat trapped in the insanity of retail and battle with it over and over. The myriad of sale items, coupons, special sales, and being open daily perplex me, annoy me, unsettle me, and even anger me at times.

When I applied for my job, I needed work as we were new to our city and state, and we just needed to get jobs. I no longer wanted to teach music privately as I had done for so many years, and for the time being, I would take what I could find. However, I did, and do, have certain goals and time I want to spend on other things, and I had a certain schedule in mind that I could accept and work with, whatever job I found. I took my job with the understanding and agreement between my boss and myself that I would not work weekends, most especially Sundays. I also made it clear that I needed a job with daytime hours only. I was very adamant about what I wanted and would accept. To my surprise, I was hired under the agreement that I would work days only and no weekends, except an occasional Saturday. My boss respected my wishes, and for the most part, I have received what I was promised, with an occasional need to remind those who do the scheduling. My schedule has, a couple of times, been a source of conflict between myself and others who were not hired under the same agreement, but I have stuck to my original request and do not feel guilty about it. I am free to have Saturdays off with my husband, and I am free to attend worship on Sundays and participate in the ways that we do. I am free to participate in musical performances we do. I am very fortunate to have this schedule; however, I was not prepared for having to work on holidays. Each holiday comes, and our store, along with many others, is open. The only day of the year my place of employment closes is Christmas Day. Comparing this to what the world was like when I was growing up and the fact that working on these days goes against my very nature and priorities, I struggle with this frequently and deeply.

"Why must stores be open on these special days?" I ask over and over. "Why is New Year's Day not a day to quietly welcome a new year and make new plans and goals for ourselves? Why are Lincoln's birthday and Washington's birthday not days to reflect on our country and the men who led it and made such a difference? Why is Easter not a day to set aside for praise and worship of our living Lord, who conquered death? Why are Memorial Day and Veteran's Day not set aside to take time to remember those who have fought and died for our freedoms? Why is the Fourth of July not a day to stop and celebrate our country? Why is Labor Day not a day to cease from labor and honor all those who do labor? Why is Thanksgiving not a day set aside to give thanks and think about all we have to be grateful for? Why are Christmas Eve and Christmas Day not days to totally stop and think of the gift God gave us?" Christmas is the one day when most of the world does stop for a moment. It is the one day I can count on being off. For some, it is about Jesus's birth; for others, it is family time and gifts. For some, it is all of that. I asked though, "Why have all these days been turned into shopping days, with everything we used to celebrate for what it is truly about now celebrated with shopping?" The only answer I know is greed and competition. There are two sides to this. On one side are the retailers who open their doors and entice shoppers with sales. On the other side are those who are sucked into shopping on those days, with both sides perpetuating what I see as a problem and the love of money and love of possessions. Even if shopping for legitimate needs, couldn't it wait a day, even if the shopper has to pay a little more?

I worked Thanksgiving Day this year. I did not want to, but it was not one of my protected Saturdays or Sundays, and I said I would. I only had to work half a day, which was appreciated. My coworkers and I did our best to be festive and enjoy our time together while working. We were there only because retail makes itself available to those who forgot groceries they feel they need or decide they wanted. Since the store was open, they came. If the store was closed, they would not come. They would have no choice but to make do. I wonder, "Why can we not plan ahead to have what we need and not need a store on a holiday?" If we do end up without something, is it really much of a tragedy? Not in my opinion. In fact, not having the option to go out would grant rest and peace. Since when do retailers need to cater to the whims of those who suddenly think of some item they decide they need? Why must retailers and shoppers perpetuate continual shopping? The love of money and the love of having more is so often the bottom line. It is my goal, purpose, and prayer to never ever make money the bottom line, to never make it my sole reason for any decision.

William Barclay wrote in his *Daily Celebration* book that advertisers used to put out ads addressing the actual needs of people. He goes on to say that advertising changed over time, and retailers began to advertise in a way to not just meet a need but to create a need. Advertising became a tool to convince us that we needed things we did not have. Most of what we see advertised today is far beyond actual need. It is about possession and greed. Retailers and advertisers set out to lure us to spend money and buy beyond our means. They created a monster in many of us that longs for more and bigger and better, or so we think. They have brainwashed us in a way. Many feel they have less value if they do not own a house, a car, the newest gadgets, or the nicest and newest fashions. It list goes on and on as to what we are convinced we need or "should" have. I have come to find all of that thinking ridiculous.

I learned early on that we can become consumed by want. When I was in my twenties, I found myself trying to keep up with friends who were spending money decorating their homes and buying new clothes and things for their children. It seemed their homes were nicer than mine, and I felt inferior in some ways. I also felt I was not doing enough to be able to buy things that I was made to feel I should want and have. I made a plan to buy one item a month, starting with throw pillows that I felt would spruce up the furniture. I started making a list of what I would buy and what I felt we needed to make our home nice and in line with everyone else. I guess it was sort of a "keeping up with the Joneses" type of thinking. However, two things become apparent. One, I was unable to achieve the financial needs to meet the goals I set for my planned purchases. Two, I didn't even really care so much about those things, and decorating was definitely not an interest for me. I felt it should be, but it wasn't. I liked my home clean, neat and tidy, and comfortable, but I just wasn't into decorating, the latest colors, etc. One day, I came to the realization that I was putting out so much effort trying to keep up, plan, and scheme that it was consuming my time and mental energy. It occurred to me that these material goals were zapping my energy and consuming my thoughts much more than they should be. I was trying to live beyond my means, and I was trying to be someone I wasn't. Why? Because society and advertisers had convinced me I needed certain things and was inferior for not having them. I was letting myself be robbed of contentment. One day, when the light bulb came on for me, I told God no longer would I worry about what seemed like such trivial things and no longer would I invest such time and energy into acquiring more just to have more and to have what is perceived as better. That was a freeing moment and decision and a very freeing day for me. A burden was lifted off my shoulders, and I became content with what I had and did not continue to strive for more. Of course, at times something needed replaced, or we may have bought a new item, but I felt I had learned a lesson and put things in perspective. I also quit trying to be someone I was not. It is very freeing when we discover who we are and who God made us to be. That can be a lifelong process.

As my coworkers and I worked together on Thanksgiving Day, a number of customers remarked how surprised they were that the store was open, and they frowned at the idea, yet they were there taking advantage of the open doors for whatever their need was. Some seemed to feel guilty about it, but they were there. Our doors were open because of them, for them. Many customers told us they were so sorry we had to work on Thanksgiving Day and gave us sad looks on our behalf. Yet there they were, shopping. The store was open because those in charge knew shoppers would come and knew they could make money on that day. In our town, there is quite a competition between the two town grocery stores. Interestingly, one coworker looked at me and stated she had been okay when she arrived at work and had come to terms with working on Thanksgiving Day. Her family had worked dinnertime out to accommodate her, but as so many customers told her they were sorry the store was open and so sorry she had to work on Thanksgiving Day, she began to feel bad and upset to have to be there. If they were going to come, she wished they would stop feeling sorry for her because now she was starting to feel sorry for herself. She commented she was going to write a letter to the editor of the newspaper, and I commented I was going to write about it as well. I wondered, "Would it really matter if the other store made more money than ours did on the holidays? Wouldn't we be better off than they for having different priorities?"

I understand that we need hospitals operating and maybe a pharmacy open. I understand maybe we need some transportation, maybe. But do we really need stores open on holidays and special days? Have we lost all sight of priorities? It has become our society's motto to accommodate every whim. It is also the practice of retail in our society to purposefully entice us to shop when we might not otherwise. It seems to have become every retailer's goal to make as much money as possible, at every chance possible, no matter the cost. There is a cost. When we put the wrong things first in our lives and hearts, there is always a cost.

It is not likely that one person can make any difference, yet it is my personal goal to refrain from shopping on holidays. It's a matter of principle for me. If I can help it, I will not enter a store. I will not be found shopping on Black Friday, frantically grabbing gifts. If at all possible, I will not be working on holidays. As long as I do work in retail, there is only so much choice I have in the matter, but I plan ahead and try to arrange those days off. If I could have our store and all stores close, I would. I will continue to voice my opinion. It is only my personal conviction, but I will strive to make every special day and holiday mean something more than shopping.

The Sky Above

Each and every day, I am amazed by the sky above me. I'm not sure when my infatuation with the sky began, but every day—morning, noon, and night—I look above. I suppose there are those who have been in love with the sky for many years. Astronomers, astronauts, and weather reporters all chose professions connecting them with the sky. Like many children, for a while, I wanted to be an astronaut when I grew up. Of course, I am not. Only a few can rise to that adventure. In college, I had a course on weather and found it rather interesting. Still, my love for the sky was on a slow simmer and, only in recent years, has become full blown. I have often been a late bloomer, it seems, and maybe it just took me more time than some to realize the beauty and the versatility of the sky. These days, each and every morning, I find the first thing I do is look out the window and look up at the sky. Aside from the beauty, there is much the sky can tell us.

The back of our house faces east, and seeing as how the sun comes up in the east, I tend to look out the back windows in the morning. I look out the front and west more often in the evenings. I have a fairly good view both directions and have seen some beautiful sunrises as well as sunsets. The photos in my computer will prove I have been moved enough times to snap many pictures of the brilliant colors I see. At night, I have often observed the moon rising in the east, and by early morning hours, I see it looming large out the front windows. Whether it is day or night, the sky is always telling us something and always intriguing with its many faces and beauty.

One thing in the sky I love to observe are the clouds. So many clouds and different types of clouds. When I was a child, I remember my father telling me about clouds. As one who is interested in the sky and the stars, my dad is an amateur astronomer and often showed me and my siblings the stars. He, at times, also took small groups of people stargazing. I remember trips to the planetarium as well. On one particular day when my father was driving me to a friend's house for an overnight stay, he pointed out the clouds to me. He proceeded to tell me what kind of clouds they were and told me about other clouds as well. On that ride, I learned about cumulus clouds, cirrus clouds, stratus clouds, and nimbus clouds. I also learned about combinations of each. I was nine years old, but I remember that ride to my friend's and what my dad taught me that day. Maybe that was the seed that later sprouted and grew into this infatuation with clouds and the sky in general.

Where we live, in the Central Northern United States, it seems there are many clouds. We have a big sky, and it spreads wide and far over us with much to see. Many days, particularly in the summer and spring, the clouds abound in the sky. There are many cumulus clouds, then, often, we suddenly have nimbus clouds, and we get a rainstorm. The weather can change quickly here during all seasons, and one need only to watch the sky and notice the changes to have a good idea of what weather is coming. There is a beauty in blue sky with white billowy clouds floating peacefully above. There is also an ominous beauty in huge, dark foreboding storm clouds and the rain, lightning, and thunder that come with them. Weather can be calm and peaceful or very threatening but always interesting and even wondrous. There is such variety in the sky if one will only look up and notice.

In the winter, the sky has many faces. There are days with a sunny blue sky and white clouds but still bitter cold. The sunshine can be deceiving. The clearest days are often the coldest with no cloud cover to warm us. There are days when the sky is all clouds, and the whole world is in shades of gray, white, and silver. It's stunning. At night, we may look up to see a clear sky with bright shining stars and moon or a cloud-covered sky barely letting the moon shine through, if at all. One of the most interesting skies of all is a night sky full of white snow clouds. Under certain weather conditions, rather than the night looking dark and black, requiring you to turn on an outside light to see, the white snow-filled clouds above along with the white snow-covered ground below cause the middle of the night to look light, almost like early daylight. At a time when it should be pitch-black outside, it is not, and you can see rather clearly. When I observe a night like that, I know before long we may have a snowfall.

Not long ago, while walking to work one morning, right in front of me the entire walk was the moon. It hung in the morning sky in the west, big and bold and utterly breathtaking. I wondered if others were seeing this striking moon. So often, we forget to look up and see what's up there above us. It was rather low, so it wasn't too difficult to notice. I asked my boss, who arrived at work about the same time I did, if he had seen the moon. He had not. I urged him to hurry and go take a look because it was such a sight to behold. Another night recently, while talking with my dad on the phone, I sat looking out the backdoor window. Suddenly, the moon, big as it could be, came up over the little hill east and slightly north of us. It was a full moon low on the horizon and was behind some trees silhouetted against a dark blue night sky. Gorgeous sight! I told my dad about it and, after our call, tried to get a few photos. Nothing compares to seeing it with the naked eye, however, and I am glad I looked into the sky that night. Later, the moon went in and out of clouds as they covered it up off and on. It was a good night to watch the moon. A few nights later, I awoke at our dog's bark to go out, and I got to see a white, light night. The snow clouds were above, and it looked like daylight. What a treat to see that. I was glad the dog needed an extra trip out. By morning, I may not have seen the exact same sight.

Last summer, while driving home from our daughter's wedding, which had taken place in another state, we saw a spectacular sky. We knew we had a thunderstorm ahead and could see rain and all kinds of cloud formations around us and in front of us. One of our sons had decided to ride home with us and visit for ten days and got to observe it all too. The sky around us was huge and wide open with so much visibility. We saw a sky more breathtaking than we had seen yet. Right on cue, as we arrived in our town and pulled into our driveway, a huge thunderstorm broke loose. It was such a gift. The storm was a great welcome home and an experience our son had not had in many years, if ever. It was a glorious homecoming, and our cameras were busy capturing the rain and lightning for a few minutes, then we settled in and watched it. It was exciting and fun to have such weather.

On summer mornings, it is common to awake to sunshine and blue sky and those billowy cumulus clouds. On those days, you'll feel warmth from the sun, whereas in the winter, we awake to the sound of snowplows clearing streets in the dark so people can later get to work. In the summer, we awake to breezes and birds singing. Each and every season has its own sky, yet it can and does change. Blue sky and white clouds give way to wind and storm clouds with thunderstorms or snow storms. Clear, cold, blue-black skies give way to a sky covered in white snow clouds and light nights then gray, silvery days often with snowfall.

There is much to see up above us. There is the sun, the moon, the stars, the clouds—all types of clouds. There are sunrises and sunsets. There is lightning. There are rainbows. In our area, there are sun dogs, and on occasion, even the northern lights can be seen. There is rainfall, sleet, hail, and snowfall. All coming from the sky. In the mild months, there are birds flittering around in the sky. In the colder months, there are geese and ducks flying over to their new destination. This year, there was a day when I got to watch the geese flying overhead. There were many flocks of them flying in formation and honking along the way. What a treat to watch them. Had I not looked up, I would have missed that sight.

Each and every day, as I awake, I will look out my windows to see what the sky has to show me. During the day, I will look up again and again, and at night, I will look again. The sun, the moon, the stars, the clouds—the sky above has much information, intrigue, and beauty to offer us.

Yesterday, we had a blizzard. It was the perfect day to sit and write my thoughts. We knew an arctic blast was approaching, and we knew the temperature was going to drop drastically. By midafternoon, we had blizzard warnings and a blizzard. I found myself often looking out the door and at the sky. All the windows were frosted or frozen over, both the storm windows and the inside windows, so to see outside, we had to open our doors and look. The storm was a tantalizing

sight. Strong wind, blowing snow, and frigid temperatures greeted my husband and me each time we took
a look outside. The sky was a solid white-gray, seen
through swirling snow. I wondered how we could feel
so safe and warm when, just inches away, on the other
side of our house's walls, a blizzard was taking place.
If outside, you would perish quickly. I quietly thanked
God for the walls and roof protecting us, for his love
and care, and also for the fantastic storm that only he
could produce and cause to cease. It did cease some
six to seven hours later. As blizzards go, it was a mild
one, still a blizzard but not as terrifying and deadly as
some can be. I took one last look outside as I headed
for bed. The wind had died down a little. As always,
my eyes went toward the sky. It was black and crystal
clear, full of twinkling stars. "Wow!" I thought. "What
a change from just a few hours ago." The sky looked
peaceful. Because it was clear, I knew the night would
be very cold, frigid cold. It was. We awoke to negative fourteen degrees, it having already warmed up a
few degrees from the night. The sky was blue and clear,
and a cold day was in store. The high temperature for
the day would never even reach zero degrees. In just
twenty-four hours, the sky had shown us many faces.
I'll be watching it to see what face it shows next.

Savoring the Moments

We all have a past, live in the present, and have a future yet to come. Many wish they could go back to earlier days. Days when they were younger and the world was different. Days they consider better days. The present is something we all deal with daily and are living in. We may find it challenging, boring, exciting, or depressing. Many just want time to pass to get on to the next thing. The future is something we plan for but have no guarantee of having. We can plan, but there is a saying: "Life is what happens while you're making other plans." It is true.

Many have a past they wish they could change or at least forget. Some have a past they wish they could return to. Most of us wish some of both. In either case, we can learn from what we wish had been different, but we can also relive special and significant moments.

Both are beneficial. Some would say they wish they couldn't remember certain hurtful things in their past or mistakes made, but on the other hand, it is our memory that lets us relive the moments we enjoyed. Many of us, as we age, long for what we consider "the good old days."

An interesting thing about time and passing years is that the young yearn to be older and the old often wish to be younger. What child is not eager to reach another birthday and get a year older? There is status and esteem attached to growing older when you're a child. You somehow feel you gain more worth with each new birthday. The opposite is often true for an older person. How many adults want to ignore their birthdays and won't tell their age? How many want to stay young or go back to earlier days. There is loss associated with growing older. There is some true loss, but much is a matter of attitude. When I was young—a teenager, I think—I remember my father, who has had great influence on me, telling me that every age is a good age. I think I had asked him about being his age, and we were discussing birthdays. I have never forgotten his statement and have found it to be true. There are good things about every age. I believe that, so far anyway, and I am well into middle age and more, depending on how long I may live. I am old enough to have things in my past I wish had been different, yet I have precious memories too and don't want to forget them. I am intrigued and amazed by life and people who have lived before me. I sometimes feel I was born one hundred years late, yet these are the years God gave me, and I cherish them and find value in life in my century too.

I can remember as far back as preschool age. I have just a few spotty memories, yet I have one mental snapshot of me sitting on some stairs with a family friend we kids called Aunt Ethel and she giving me a black oriental jewelry box that plays music. I am pretty certain she gave it to me and that I was three years old. I still have that jewelry box. It is amazing that it has followed me all these years. I cherish it because it is special piece of my childhood and the woman who was part of it. I do remember, however, as a grade school child, envying a friend who had a jewelry box with a dancing ballerina. We decided one day that we would trade jewelry boxes, and I gave her my oriental-looking box, and she gave me her dancing ballerina box. I brought it home feeling rather guilty and sheepish about it. As it is with mothers, my mom knew something was up and came looking for me. She saw my guilty look and found out about the switch in jewelry boxes then made me go return the dancing ballerina and retrieve my black oriental box. I don't actually know why it mattered that we traded, if we both wanted to, but my mother saw something in me she did not like, I think, and made me undo the trade. Today, I am so grateful for whatever insight she had about that trade. Maybe she didn't like that fact that I was envious. Maybe she liked my box better. Maybe she remembered who had given it to me. I don't know, but at my age today, I cherish that special box, and I am grateful to my mom for making me get it back. The box lives in my hope chest, where I keep spe-

cial things, and it holds certain jewelry pieces of years
gone by, mostly things I had as a child. If my memory
is correct, I have had that box almost fifty-four years.
It isn't the box itself that is so special, though it is an
extremely unique box. I have never seen one like it. But
it is the long-ago memory and the people who were
in my life associated with the box. I might be much
older now, but all of that is still part of me and the life
given me; I have many memories of childhood. I hold
on to them tightly as they all had something to do with
who I am today. Those were good years. They were years
when it was fun to have a birthday and grow older. They
were years full of learning and experiencing so much.
Each grade school year was a fun age as I look back.

The teen years were a bit different. They were more
difficult in some ways but also more exciting as more
freedom was given and as boyfriends came into the
picture. I don't remember too many horrific moments
from my teen years. There were a few. I enjoyed school
and had friends both at school and at church. My time
was filled with schoolwork and time with friends. I
was given a lot of freedom, it seems. There was a time
when my freedom was taken away, and it was the
first and only time I can remember being grounded.
I had directly disobeyed my mom and dad and gone
straight to a boy's house where I was not allowed to go.
Basically, I lied or was deceitful, but as usual, just like
with the music box, I was caught immediately. There is
something about my personality that cannot break one
single tiny rule without being caught and having significant consequences. I learned that fairly early on. When

others could lie, sneak, or break rules and get away with it, I absolutely could not. I don't know why, but I am sure it protected me from harm. I still cannot get away with anything and don't try. I don't want to. On the few occasions I did try as a teenager, I was caught right away. I was a bit at odds with my parents during my eighth-grade year, and of course, I thought I understood life better than they, but when I got grounded, I was struck with great remorse. I spent a number of weeks and maybe months trying to make it up to my parents. I don't know if they noticed my efforts, but I really wanted to be trusted and worked hard to prove I was trustworthy. The experience of being restricted and losing my parents' trust made a lifelong impact on me. That kind of thing is not what I wanted in my life, and I set out to do better. I remember my teen years basically as good years, even with the struggles a child that age encounters. They were good years in their own way. You gain some freedom and have a lot of fun but don't have adult responsibilities yet.

When I was a teenager, I looked at young adults in their mid-twenties and decided twenty-five was the perfect age. I remember thinking to be twenty-five must be great. At twenty-five, you are an adult and old enough to make your own choices, have your own home, be married, and have children. Wow, to be twenty-five must be perfect. You are still young but all grown up. I reached twenty-five, and I did enjoy those years. At twenty-five, I was married and had two children and had another on the way soon. My twenties were full of pregnancies, babies, and diapers, and all that goes with being a young mother. I look back now and wonder where on earth I got the energy to handle all that. At twenty-five, you have energy. Would I choose to be twenty-five again? Absolutely not, though those were special years. I have many special memories of my children, and certain ones stick strongly in my mind.

When our oldest was not quite two and was learning the names of so many things, I remember a day when we were in the car, Jason in his car seat, and he pointed his little finger toward the sky and said, "Bird" as a bird flew by. I was so excited. I can remember the joy I felt at him putting that together and naming the creature he saw fly across the sky. It is a moment forever in my heart. Or the days he and I sat on the floor playing, and I watched as he worked hard to put certain-shaped toy pieces into the corresponding hole that only that shape would fit. It was fascinating to watch him try and learn. He was a quiet baby and a quiet child, mostly keeping his thoughts to himself but always observing and thinking. Jason is a hardworking man today, highly skilled at a trade he has worked in many years. He is still fairly quiet, very observant, thoughtful, and very generous. He goes about his life without drawing much attention to himself but is often found helping others.

Our second son was born, and from birth, he was curious about things. I will never forget his eyes immediately after birth—open wide and looking around. It was a clue to his personality, not to mention how much he had kicked before birth. When he was one month old, I sat rocking him to sleep as I caught sight of the two of us in the closet door mirrors. There he was, totally relaxed and asleep in my arms, a tiny boy with no cares. I stared at our image and at the wonder of how this tiny babe was so trusting of me as I held him. He had no worries or fear. I suddenly felt an overwhelming responsibility to him and wanted to protect him forever. I looked at how much he had grown in just one month, and I cried because he was already so old. His first month was gone. It was only eight more months, and he was off and running. We were playing outside one day when, suddenly, he stood up and walked across the yard. I was shocked. He was so little and so young. True to his first moments after birth, Ryan has always been curious and into things. We took him out of his crib because he kept climbing out, and we were afraid he would fall and get hurt. He climbed onto counter tops and ate things off the ground. He was a child always on the go, curious and full of energy and always entertaining. Ryan's curiosity and go-getter personality has allowed him to achieve many goals—both in jobs and schooling. He is always on an adventure and he still keeps us entertained and laughing.

Amy, our daughter, came along after two boys. I was very happy with boys, but I longed for a daughter since I already had two boys. With everything in me, I asked God for a daughter. My doctor knew my strong desire was for a girl, and as she was born, he said, "You're going to be happy with this baby. You have a daughter." My first memory of Amy is of the doctor handing her to me right after her birth and Amy immediately trying to suckle. She was always a hungry one. One of her first words was "more," wanting more food as she sat in her high chair. What struck me about baby Amy was how different she looked as a baby than her brothers had as infants. I didn't realize till then that girls' bodies look very different than boys, even at birth. Her hips where shaped differently, and she had more fat on her, though she didn't weigh any more than her brothers had at birth. She looked very different, and she looked like a girl. One of my deeply embedded memories of Amy is when she was two to three years old and I became very ill with influenza. I was very sick and in bed. The boys were old enough for school, but Amy was home with me, sick as I was. She would come to me, lay beside me, pat my arm, and say, "Okay, Mommy? It's okay." And she would stay near me. Thankfully, she did not get sick. Amy has always been full of compassion and has always looked out for others. When she was a young girl, she would become distressed when she saw homeless people on the street, a common sight in the city where we lived. One day, as I took her to McDonald's for lunch, she was concerned about a homeless man standing outside and wouldn't rest till we bought him some food. He took the food we offered and ate. I have no idea how many meals that man may have gotten, maybe many, maybe few, but Amy was moved to feed that man and we did. Today, she is highly trained and educated in a field that helps adults in need. The moments I savored when my children were young gave clues to who they would become as adults.

All the years the kids were growing up were full and busy and challenging, at times problematic and exhausting, but those were good years just as the previous years had good and significance to them. There was laughter and tears through all those years and major challenges each of us faced, yet they were special years in their own way. Each year and age offered something. As time has passed and I have reached middle age, I certainly don't have the energy I did in those earlier years, but I have other things. Though I still work, I have more time to myself. I have more time to pursue hobbies and interests. We gained a daughter-in-law and had a granddaughter along the way, and for a time, I had a baby to hold again. She is no longer a baby. Babyhood is long gone again. We have gained a son-in-law and another grandchild. He was born the same year and just two days after our granddaughter. My children are now adults, each having found their own path. Children grow up and parents grow older. Time has moved on.

It's a different time now, and there are some adjustments. Bodies change, at least to some degree. Energy levels lessen some. Interests have changed to some degree. I'm less busy in some ways but just as content, or more so. Age brings some wisdom, hopefully, and there is less striving than when we are younger. At times, I miss some things from the past, but I would not choose to go back. Memories provide us with those moments to relive and talk about. I try every day to enjoy each moment, knowing now how fast they go by. Each day is one to be cherished, and I find it important to live in the now, as the saying goes. Any time I feel myself start to wish my time away, wishing I could get on to the next thing or at least get past what I am doing, I stop myself and remember to savor every moment.

That has become my motto, savor the moments. We have our past and our memories, we have the present to enjoy, but we do not know how much future we have or what it will be. I don't want to miss the blessings and significance of each day. I want to appreciate each day. My age now is enjoyable, just as past days were. Each age is enjoyable for a different reason. There are many things to experience and appreciate at every age if we stop to look and think about it. Small things can bring great pleasure these days. A phone call, loving message or letter in the mailbox from a friend or family member, a walk outside in any weather, snuggling with a pet, a good book to read, or hobby to work on. Time with friends. Sitting home in a comfortable house with one you love at the end of a day and after a work week. Solitude, which was harder to come by in earlier, busier years.

I watch and admire those older than myself. I observe many still enjoying life even in their nineties. Some still drive. Some walk to where they want to go. Many still shop for themselves. Most are grateful for each day. We are all a work in progress no matter what our age. We all go through trials, struggles, failures, and defeat. It has been true for me and each one in my family. Not every decision or experience was perfect or easy or felt good, yet those are not what we focus on. We choose to focus on our successes and growth. In every struggle, we can do our best with it and leave the rest to God, casting all our cares on him as the Bible says in 1 Peter 5:7. As long as we live, we can learn and grow and have God-given joy in every situation.

God gave each one of us a certain number of days to live, and none of us knows how many days we have. In all stages of life, God gives pleasure and gifts for that age. In all parts of life, he equips us for what we need to do and accomplish and for whatever he may ask of us. For this reason, all ages are a good age as we accept the specialness of each. If we are given the chance to live through many years and stages of life, then we need only to embrace each day and each year and ask God for his grace in each and ask what we may do in each stage to further his work and his message through us. God can bless us and use us at any age if we are willing. Babyhood, childhood, adolescence, young adult years, middle age years, senior years, and old age, all are years of significance. Each has special blessings and special challenges, and the joy of each is ours as we savor the moments.

Afterword

It is in the quietest moments when I hear God whisper to me. It is one reason I seek quiet moments. *Mornings on the Porch* is about quiet or special moments when I heard God or felt his holy presence. It is about the details of our lives that he is in if only we will be still and look and listen. Many of these realizations came to me as I sat quietly on my porch in the early mornings, drinking my cup of cocoa and pondering life, as I watched our neighborhood wake up.

There are many ways God reaches out to us. If we will quiet ourselves and watch and listen we will see him and hear him. In our sorrows and joys we can find him. In the most ordinary or mundane of days we can find him. Sometimes we might not realize he is there until we look back and see that he was. God is interested in every detail of our life. He is interested in what matters to us.

Mornings on the Porch is stories from my life when I have experienced God's presence and blessings, love and care, teachings and guidance. In sharing them, I hope you will also recognize God's presence in your own life, how he cares for you and what he wants to teach you. It matters because we matter to him and he wants to bless us abundantly if we will allow ourselves to know him.

—Nancy

Nancy Kuykendall studied music and taught music for thirty years, most specifically the piano, but also bass guitar and soprano recorder. Nancy ran a private teaching studio, as well as taught music in a private school for ten years. She has played piano for churches and a wide variety of events throughout the years. She met and married her musician husband during those years, and the two have been performing together throughout their marriage.

After retiring from teaching, Nancy took up writing. Her inspiration comes from her experiences, surroundings, circumstances, life events, and the people and pets in her life. *Mornings on the Porch* is Nancy Kuykendall's first book.

Nancy has three adult children: Jason, Ryan and Amy. She makes her home in North Dakota with her husband Steve, their English bulldog Melody, and their silver tabby cat Merri.

Aside from writing, Nancy spends time in music performance and enjoys knitting, crochet, reading, photography, and fitness walking.